Ableton Live 6

TIPS AND TRICKS

Martin Delaney

PC Publishing

PC Publishing
Keeper's House
Merton
Thetford
Norfolk IP25 6QH
UK

Tel +44 (0)1953 889900
Fax +44 (0)1953 889901
email info@pc-publishing.com
website http://www.pc-publishing.com

First published 2007

© PC Publishing

ISBN 13: 978 1906005 023

All rights reserved. No part of this publication may be reproduced or transmitted in any form, including photocopying and recording, without the written permission of the copyright holder, application for which should be addressed to the Publishers. Such written permission must also be obtained before any part of this publication is stored in an information retrieval system of any nature.

British Library Cataloguing in Publication Data
A catalogue record for this book is available from the British Library

Printed and bound in Great Britain by Cromwell Press, Trowbridge, Wilts

Contents

Introduction
A manual, a tip, a trick...what's the difference? Live does everything you want it to – you just don't know it yet! Who is this book for? Learning curve of enlightenment - or twisted pretzel of confusion? The test rig.

1 **What's new (and old) in Live 6?** *1*
What is Live? Who is it for? How do they use it? What's new in Live 6?

2 **Get organised** *11*
Installation. Mac or PC? System requirements. Check for updates. Cracks. Another use for Demo Mode. Managing your computer resources. What hardware do you need? Signal routing ins and outs. Do the lessons. Shortcuts. Configuring with audio/MIDI hardware. Managing files and sets. Keeping file sizes down. Templates. The Browser. The Library. Moving to Live 6? Ten top transitional tips.

3 **Managing files and sets** *21*
Loading sets or parts of sets into another set. Look at the library. Collect all and save. What lurks in the project folder?

4 **Clips and scenes and a little on tracks** *25*
Clips in general. Nudge. Groove. Unlinking clip envelopes. Consolidation. Follow actions rule! Live clips. Audio clips. MIDI clips. Scenes. Song header scenes. Routing audio between tracks. Sending audio to return tracks. Audio from one track to many. Audio from many tracks to one. It works with MIDI too – from one track to many, and from many tracks to one.

5 **Devices** *45*
Audio effects. MIDI effects. Instruments. Device racks. Device delay compensation.

6 **Sampling in Live** *53*
Audio clips. Simpler. Impulse. Sampler. Hot-Swapping samples.

7 **Automation** *57*
Clip automation in general. MIDI clip automation. Audio clip automation. Automating the cross fader. Envelopes in tracks – the Arrangement View. Versatile envelopes. Envelopes in the library.

8 **About the views** *65*
Left brain, right brain!

9   Live talks to itself 67
Send MIDI from Live to – Live. Song setup clips. The MIDI mangler.

10   Performance notes 75
Live is an instrument – really. A set for every song, or every song in the set? Prepare your set for performance. Song header scenes. Onstage troubleshooting. Device racks in a live situation. Solo performance – J-Lab. Jamming. Using Live within a band – Songcarver/Keith Lang. Jamming in the Arrangement View is just wrong. Live in the theatre. VJing - video performance alongside Live.

11   DJing notes 87
Why is Live good for DJs? Live DJing with Jody Wisternoff (Way Out West). Pre listening/Cueing. MIDI hardware setup. Live DJing with Tarekith. Manage your song folders. Pre analysis. Warping entire songs. Tap tempo. Live DJing with John 00 Fleming.

12   Studio notes 93
Songwriting. Jen Bloom. Remixes and mashups with Live. Build a 16-step sequencer.

13   Movie notes 103
Movie soundtracks with Live. Locators. Exporting it all together. ReWire to another DAW. Frank Blum.

14   Teaching notes 107
How to get somebody hooked on Live. In the classroom with Live.

15   Using Live with other software and hardware 111
ReWire. Live and Reason – somebody has to be in charge. ReWiring Live to other sequencers. Down another Mac-only alley – ReWiring Live to GarageBand. Arkaos VJ. MIDI Time Code and MIDI Clock.

16   Using Live with hardware keyboards and controllers 123
Less is more. The Kenton Killamix Mini. Trigger Finger. Behringer FCB1010. Mackie Control Universal. M-Audio Ozonic. Jazz Mutant Lemur. Going Wireless – the Nintendo Wii Remote Control. Not actually MIDI – the Griffin PowerMate. Live's pseudo-MIDI keyboard.

17   Using Live with audio and MIDI interfaces 132
Echo AudioFire2 pocket-sized FireWire audio/MIDI interface. Edirol FA-66 FireWire compact audio/MIDI interface. Combo audio/MIDI interfaces/controllers. Live and multiple audio interfaces.

18   Get more sounds 135
Samples on disc. Online samples. Apple Loops. Reason Refills. Live with Stylus RMX. Trackteam Audio Livefills. Ableton Live Packs. Operator. Record your own. External sound generators. External DSP cards.

19   Live Packs 141

20   Links 143

21   Top ten keyboard shortcuts 147

Index 149

A manual, a tip, a trick, what's the difference?

RTFM, people say on the internet, Read The F****** Manual; quite a rude way to make a valid point. And now – it's my turn to say to you – as nicely as possible – RTFM!

Ableton Live 6 Tips and Tricks is *not* intended to be a rehash of the Live manual, which you already have on your computer in PDF form, accessible via 'Read the Live Manual' in the Live Help menu (if you bought a boxed copy of Live, you have a printed copy too – and some cool stickers). Although there's inevitable crossover with the Live documentation, the things in this book have arisen through experimentation and experience (and, sometimes, asking other people). Amongst other things, this book's about how Live interacts with the user, and with the outside world, in the form of musicians, other computers, peripherals, and almost-essentials such as audio/MIDI interfaces and hardware controllers. As the old saying goes, 'No Live user is an island'.

Ableton Live isn't a regular DAW – Digital Audio Workstation (pronounced 'door' – horrible, isn't it?) – and anything written about it has to reflect that. It's common to play software instruments within Cubase or Logic, but, although Live also hosts software instruments in various forms, it can be considered an instrument in its own right.

Live does everything you want it to – you just don't know it yet

Whenever it's possible, I work exclusively with Live – getting to know it better, and using workrounds to achieve results that would otherwise need other software/hardware. You might be surprised at what this simple-looking software can manage with a bit of deviousness.

Who is this book for?

The newcomer: if you're in the early Live-curious stages of use, this book will give you a kick-start with some of the concepts and applications that are possible with Live, saving you weeks of fiddling, probing, and head-scratching, so you can get to the sweet stuff ASAP. It's not the same as the manual.

For the intermediate user: This book will introduce you to Live features that you might not have encountered yet – maybe you've been too busy, or maybe you've got too comfortable in those cosy old ways, unaware of the thrills that recent updates bring. It's not the same as the manual.

For the advanced user: As well as showing you new features and nutty ideas, I've included reminders of more commonly-known Live features. Some of these reminders involve stating the obvious – I don't know about you, but sometimes I need that. There are so many things to learn, and working habits are so easy to get into, that you just can't retain it all. And if you don't even recognise the thing I'm 'reminding' you of – just keep it to yourself and nobody will ever know...you can do the same for me some time. By the way, did I say it's not the same as...ah, now you're getting the idea!

For those using a cracked copy of Live: Do everybody a favour and buy it. Those features you're enjoying didn't just fall out of the ideas tree straight into your computer; people have invested a lot of time and creativity to bring you Live. Before pleading poverty, consider that you may qualify for an educational discount, and remember that 'Lite' versions of Live are often included with audio hardware packages, from people like M-Audio, Mackie, and Tascam, giving you a convenient all-in-one affordable way into the Live-plus-hardware experience.

Learning curve of enlightenment – or twisted pretzel of confusion?

Because Live leads a dual existence as a performance instrument and studio tool, it can be tricky to organise a book like this one; it has to be categorised somehow. Where relevant, I've put common things together – items common to all arenas of Live use. I've also used (very broad) sections to cover more specific Live activities. There's a huge amount of crossover in everything that Live does, so don't be surprised if certain features pop up in unexpected places.

There are INFO boxes dotted around, containing supplementary bits of information designed to enhance your reading experience. These boxes are generally connected to the content of the page you're reading, but more abstract comments will appear from time to time – there's one in the margin here.

The test rig

I'm a Mac user, but I've endeavoured to keep everything cross-platform in this book (with some notable exceptions). However, it might be useful for you to know what my basic set-up was while writing this book:

- Apple iMac G5 20inch, 2.1Ghz, 2GB RAM, 500GB hard drive.
- Fujitsu Siemens 20inch LCD display.
- Apple G4 PowerBook 12inch, 1.5 Ghz, 1.25 GB RAM, 80 GB hard drive.
- Lacie FireWire-bus powered hard drives.

...still holding off before making the switch to Intel.

Alongside Ableton Live, I use Logic Pro, Arkaos VJ, Arturia Moog Modular V, and the Korg Legacy Collection with MS20 controller.

For outboard hardware I use the the Kenton Killamix Mini (which I designed), 2 Griffin Technology PowerMates, Behringer FCB1010 MIDI pedalboard, Novation X-Station 25 synth/controller, and Edirol FA-66 FireWire audio interface. My bass is a horribly battered and therefore very cool 1976 Fender Jazz, which I record through a Boss GT-6B pedalboard.

Well, that's it, and thanks for coming, hope you enjoyed it. Oh! Wait! Just kidding...I hope you get something positive from reading this book; what I most want to do is encourage you to try new things with Live, to experiment...do something that you wouldn't usually do with it. Catch you later!

Info

Are you browsing through this book in the music store while your little sister shops for violin strings? Wondering what all the fuss is about? Go to www.ableton.com and download the Ableton Live demo. There are Mac OS and Windows versions, and it does everything the full version does, except save and export. It's not time-limited.

About the author

I'm still Martin Delaney; still pleased to meet you. We've been here before, haven't we?

I've been using Ableton Live since version 1.0.1, back in 2001, and I'll probably be using it until version 58.1 or I drop, whichever comes first. Before Live came along I'd played exactly *one* live show; although I'd been creating music for years, I wasn't a 'musician' – I don't really sing or play any instruments – I was just into songwriting and sequencing and making an electronic noise, so there wasn't a comfortable way for me to present my music in a live environment. Eventually I bit the bullet, and hauled my 'studio' on stage for that one gig. Although it worked okay, it was a big hassle, and not quite what I wanted to do.

Shortly after this gig, my friend Paul Wiffen (writing in *Sound On Sound*) mentioned an intriguing new software product called Ableton Live. I emailed Paul with a couple of questions, then rushed to the Ableton website and purchased my first copy of Live. At the time I was jamming at home on an iBook with dozens of QuickTime Pro files looping on screen; it was fun, but there was no easy way to organise or record what happened. I initially saw Live as a way of organising that chaos by saving my QuickTime loops in the Session View's grid. It's come a long way since then, though that jamming ability is still what makes Live work for me – I now use Live in all musical situations: performing, composing, recording, jamming, and remixing. I also teach Live on a one-to-one basis to other musicians, and to groups of students, as part of my activity with Public Loop.

My first book *Laptop Music* was published by PC Publishing, who have brought you this (revised) title too; in *Sound On Sound*, Martin Walker (obviously a man of taste) wrote: 'Overall, I loved this book's streetwise approach – it's one of the most entertaining music technology reads I've ever had, and well worth the money!'; us Martins have to stick together.

If reading my books isn't enough for you, I also teach Ableton Live 1-on-1. Book me: learnlive@mac.com. Read about my Ableton Live 101 training movies at www.macprovideo.com.

What's that you're asking? What do I do when I'm not working with Ableton Live? I, er…um…well, you keep in touch now.

Ableton Live is my instrument.

Acknowledgments

It's time to round up the usual suspects and buy them all a latte!

Personal
Jan Anderson, Carey Armstrong, my Dad and brothers, the amazing Jane Yolanda. The people I've worked with lately: 7 Seconds Of Love, mindlobster, Andi Studer at After-Dinner Recordings, Barkless Dog, Caroline Alexander at the Toilet Gallery, Dean at Miloco, Donald Tempi, Funsize Lions, Gagarin, J-Lab, Lee Mangan and the Steranko guys, Tokyo Joe, and Vic Twenty.

Extra special thanks to Julian, Elli, Miranda, and Freya – my favourite band.

For the book
Phil Chapman at PC Publishing; Alexandra at Behringer for the FCB1010; Conny and John at Edirol for the FA-66; Mathias at Faderfox for the DJ-1, LV-1, and LX-1; Colin at M-Audio for the Trigger Finger. Jody Wisternoff; the Live lab rats: J-Lab, Songcarver, Jen Bloom, Frank Blum, Tarekith and Joe Young.

At Ableton
Gerhard Behles, Ulrich Fischer, Robert Henke, Dave Hill Jr, Christian Kleine, Axel Klingelhofer, Anita Lotterschmid, Jesse Terry, and all the other Abletons. Thanks for enabling us to make music the way we always wanted to... and for keeping it on track... and for the quality control!

And...
Every friendly and curious face I meet when I'm out there with my laptop, running Ableton Live on stage, in studios, or jamming and writing in coffee shops...and everybody on AbletonLiveDJ.com!

Images/quotes
All product photos courtesy of the relevant manufacturers.
Apple hardware images courtesy of Apple.
Photos on page 110 by Martin Delaney.
J-Lab photo by Martin Delaney.
Hans Zimmer quote from the Ableton website.
See the 'Links' section at the back of the book for website addresses.

What's new (and old) in Live 6?

It's tempting to skip the entire 'what is Ableton Live and what does it do?' routine – as you've gone to the trouble of picking up this book, then you must already have some idea of what Live is about – you've purchased it, or have at least downloaded the demo. If you don't yet have Live in full or demo form, grab it from the Ableton site now. If you're a fully-functioning user of a previous version, that goes for you too – you'll be surprised at how Live has evolved. And while you're there, check for upgrade opportunities and bundle offers. And t-shirts. And bags.

But you know, maybe we should prod our collective memories; we can remind ourselves why we're here, and what our common interests are – the abiding concepts that made Live so exciting in the first place...

What is Ableton Live?

Ableton Live is the cross-platform software that changed the music world – not just the music software world. Live has gathered fans – in a way usually associated with performers rather than software – as it has matured into an

Live Session View

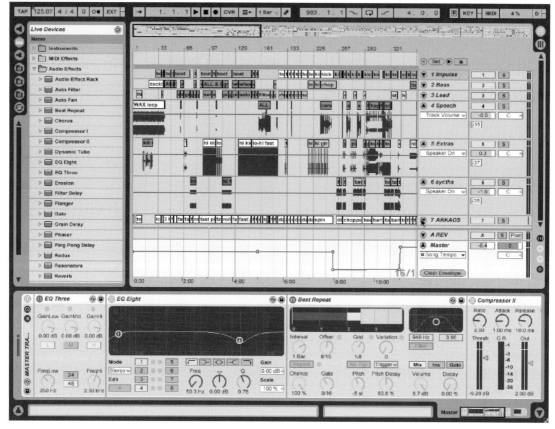

Live Arrangement View

all-powerful performance instrument and a credible alternative to established software workstations – the DAWs I mentioned in the introduction.

Live was created by Robert Henke and Gerhard Behles, beginning as a simple loop-based jamming tool with a unique interface. At a time when music software designers were continuing to produce interfaces that imitated hardware, Live looked like something derived from spreadsheet, web, and game design – which doesn't sound very 'musical', but... it is. Not only did Live allow a computer to become a sampling instrument capable of real-time performance, it retained many functions of 'traditional' music sequencing/recording, with it's two 'views' - Session and Arrangement. An instrument that records itself, but which can also record other instruments – interesting (also the cause of mucho confusion for newcomers).

Another quirk – despite its 'futuristic' nature, Live embraces some of the oldest principles of electronic music, especially those relating to sampling, with its focus on mangling chunks of sound. Live's follow actions – 'random' playback elements with a degree of user-definability – are reminiscent of generative music (especially given the chaotic possibilities I'll discuss in 'Live Talks To Itself!'), Operator includes FM-style synthesis, usually associated with the 1980s (but dating back much further), and the Arpeggiator is hardly a new concept, though imbued with typical Ableton panache.

Arpeggiator and Operator

So, here's a handy reminder of what Live does:

Session and Arrangement Views
The two faces of Live: the Session View, built for performance and jamming; and the Arrangement View, optimised for more considered song-building tasks. Whatever happens, you'll end up working in both of these views, so get used to them.

Audio and MIDI clips
These are Live's core components: audio or MIDI segments that can be recorded, edited, triggered, looped, stretched, transposed, processed, automated, and grouped (as scenes).

Warping
This is what Live's all about. The timing of an audio clip can be changed by the insertion of warp markers – a drum hit (or any part of any sound) can be moved to fall exactly on a beat or a division of a beat. You can change not only the tempo, but the rhythmic nature of any audio – altering the groove of a drum loop, or transforming a recording of a faulty air conditioning unit into a tasty rhythm part. All without stopping the song!

Time stretching algorithms for a range of material
Audio clips can be assigned individual time stretching algorithms, for instance 'Beats' or 'Tones' - though you don't have to use the 'right' one, by any means; not only doesn't the 'right' one always work best, you'll get some interesting effects by using the 'wrong' one.

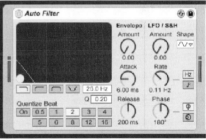

Live's Auto filter

Native, Audio Unit, and VST instruments and effects
Live includes a suite of Devices – audio effects (Auto Filter for example), MIDI effects (like Arpeggiator), and four instruments; Impulse, Simpler, Operator, and Sampler. It's also compatible with third-party Audio Unit and VST plug-ins – the Live instruments and effects can't be used directly within other sequencers.

MIDI and computer keyboard mapping options for real-time triggering
Nearly all Live functions are assignable to MIDI and computer keyboard commands, emphasising real-time control and minimising mouse work. Not only can you trigger a particular loop or activate an effect via MIDI, you can select tracks, scroll through clips, start/stop playback, and much more.

Collage style of working

Sounds from different sources (and of different formats and sample rates) can be added and manipulated in real time. Freely combine parts from software instruments, with your audio recordings, and material from CDs, the internet – the more varied the better.

MIDI recording

Work with MIDI in a linear 'sequencing' fashion in the Arrangement View, or jam with MIDI clips in the Session View. Import a MIDI file (or selected tracks from within the file), draw in notes with the pencil tool, or record notes played on Live's 'pseudo' MIDI keyboard, or via an external MIDI keyboard controller.

Drawing-in of MIDI notes

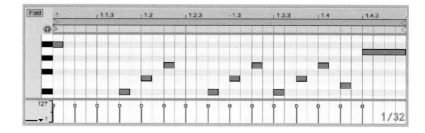

Multitrack audio recording

Record multiple audio tracks simultaneously – as many as your audio interface and your computer will tolerate, going through the entire recording process without hitting 'stop'; use MIDI to control record functions.

Example of routing options

Tap tempo

Tap tempo makes beat matching easier – useful for DJs, and Live players working alongside 'real' instruments.

Routing options

Live has the simplest routing system around – but that doesn't mean 'basic'. Audio and MIDI can be routed between tracks, and effects send/returns created, with just a few clicks. Create audio submixes and bounces, send MIDI info to different instruments simultaneously, share one processor-hungry effect (such as reverb) across several tracks.

ReWire compatibility

ReWire synchronises Live with other music software, such as Logic, Cubase, and Reason. Use it to exploit the best qualities of different applications.

> **Info – Session vs Arrangement**
>
> Some Live users don't grasp the relationship between the Arrangement and Session Views; they'll work comfortably in one view, regarding the other as a mysterious place that requires a passport and vaccinations to visit. Please explore and understand the relationship between Arrangement and Session; in time, working across them becomes second nature. It's easy enough to do – just hit the tab key!

Who is Live for? How do they use it?

Live's performance angle was the thing that initially attracted experimentalists and jammers, but since then it's been adopted by instrumentalists, DJs, remixers, producers, and composers – people working in all fields of music. They use Live because of the real-time manipulation, friendly interface, and flexibility – like a game, it encourages you to find connections and workrounds that you didn't know existed.

> **Quote**
>
> 'For me, the overall best thing about Live is its ability to manipulate audio in ways that ProTools and Logic do not possess. Changing the feel and swing of a loop by adjusting its warp points produces results that were previously unrealistic. The compositional power of Live is now on a par with Logic and Pro Tools. All this, and I haven't even mentioned its live performance features, which are unique and in a class of their own.' – *Jody Wisternoff, Way Out West*

In Live, tasks like 'performer' and 'composer' bleed into each other – the composer is now a performer, and the performer creates songs in real-time, recording his jams for subsequent refinement.

- *Composers* – create new parts and rearrange songs without ever hitting 'stop'; skip between the Session and Arrangement Views for uninterrupted stream-of-consciousness creativity.
- *Laptop jammers* – go to the club and ruthlessly dismantle your carefully-crafted studio work, or go on stage with an empty Session View, and build a soundscape as you go; record it all and burn it to CD or post it online the same night.
- *Band members* – put Live at the heart of your on-stage technology – to use a very abused phrase, it's your digital music hub!
- *Soloists, vocalists and instrumentalists* – run backing tracks, host software instruments, and process your sound in real time. Control Live from a MIDI keyboard, a MIDI pickup on your instrument, or from a MIDI pedal board.
- *Sound designers* – create evolving sound textures in real-time. Use it in the theatre to deliver sound effects and cues right on time, in a flexible way that accommodates the vagaries of live performance.
- *Soundtrack composers* – stretch your music and other audio to fit that last-minute edit. Import QuickTime movies directly into Live's Arrangement View and watch them in a separate window, or even a separate display.
- *Producers* – record multitrack audio, then manipulate it – fast – in ways that leave other DAWs in the dust.
- *Remixers* – use Live to create alternative mixes, tempos, sounds, effects, and beats. Make original tracks fit entirely different beats and tempos.
- *DJs* – use Live's auto-warping to have a stack of MP3s in your songs folder, ready to drop into your set at any time. Throw in more beats, sounds, and effects. Use Live's crossfader and Re-Pitch warp mode for old-school DJ action.

Info View and Menu item for website

Info – you need help

Hit '?' to access Live's Info View, at the bottom left of your screen, for info about the interface object you're mousing over. If that isn't enough info, next stop should be the Help menu, where you can access the lessons, Live manual, or follow a link to the website.

What's new in Live 6?

I don't want to dwell too much on the specifics of listing every new feature in Live 6, but it's worth taking a quick look, just so we're aware of what the update brings. Some of these new features will be mentioned in more detail, at the appropriate time, as we work through the following chapters.

Device racks

The device group is dead – kind of. Don't worry – if you enjoyed working with device groups in earlier versions, you'll go nuts when you see what you can do with racks, which have replaced groups (from Live 6 onwards). But don't worry – any device groups you created previously will be automatically converted to racks, so you won't lose your old favourites. If you're familiar with Reason's Combinator, I guess that's a fair comparison.

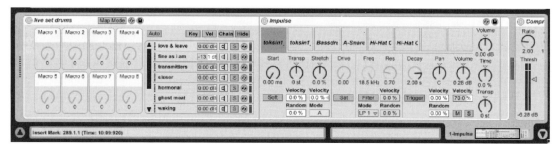

Device rack with Impulse drum sampler

New and improved audio and MIDI effect devices

EQ4 has been upgraded to EQ8; any previously-created EQ4 presets will still function within EQ8. The Dynamic Tube effect, which brings the possibility of 'warmer', more vacuum tube-like distortions, in both subtle and extreme ways, threatens to become one of the most-used of Live's devices. Saturator has been given a waveshaper with six user defined parameters, and a second optional output saturator/soft clipper. Utility's new Panorama control makes it possible to pan entire device chains. Operator has new filter modes and new FM algorithms.

On the MIDI device front, Note Length forces incoming MIDI notes to pre-determined lengths, and can also can be used to trigger new notes from note off events.

Improved ReWire support means that other ReWire master applications, such as Cubase or Logic, can now access Live's instruments directly.

Sampler

A new Live instrument: Sampler, the missing piece in the puzzle... a fully featured multisampler, capable of loading patches from the supplied Essential

Sampler's 'Sample' tab

Instrument Collection sample library (if you buy the boxed version of Live), and (even better) from other popular sample formats such as Kontakt (if non-encrypted), Akai, and EXS/GarageBand, Creative/Emu, Soundfonts, and Tascam's Gigastudio. Inevitably, this has lead to some finagling with Live's 'one window' rule, as more features are shoehorned in – the Live interface has been pushed to the limit, with some devious manoeuvres to squeeze out the necessary screen space for Sampler's many controls. Sampler is a great addition to Live's devices, and will have the intended effect – causing many users of other workstations to finally jump ship! Be aware that, although a demo of Sampler is included with Live, it's an add-on which you must pay for to obtain full functionality (just like Operator).

Sampler's zone editor

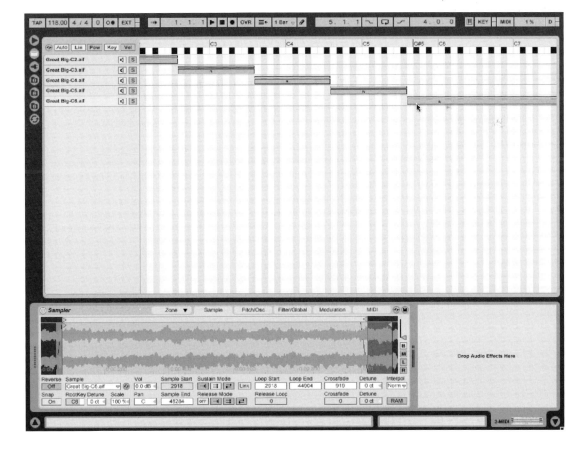

File management

File management has been substantially revised. Files or folders can now be bookmarked in the Browser. There's a Hot-Swap Browser, for swapping samples in devices. Saving a new Live set now creates a project folder, containing various sub folders for different types of sample material. Projects can be scanned for unused or missing files, and saved as Live Packs. Individual tracks can be exported (another long-awaited DAW feature). Ctrl-click in the sample display allows you to crop, discarding unused portions of the sample. AAC file import is supported, as long as the files aren't protected by Digital Rights Management – the dreaded DRM.

Resource management

A switch in Live's Preferences enables multicore and multiprocessor support. Track freezing, where audio or MIDI tracks, with their effects, are temporarily rendered to disk to save CPU usage, has been taken to a new level, enabling much more to be done, during a Live set for instance, without unfreezing a track.

QuickTime movie integration

At last... finally... Live includes QuickTime movie support, with the movie either appearing in a pop-up window or in a large window on a second display. See the 'Movie Soundtracks' chapter later.

QuickTime movie in Arrangement View

EIC instrument bundle (with boxed version)

At last... finally (again)... Live comes to terms with 'real' instruments. Pianos, electric keyboards, orchestral strings and brass, woodwinds, plucked instruments, mallets, voices... it's all in the boxed version of Ableton Live 6, which includes several GB of extras in the form of the Essential Instrument Collection (or EIC). These sample-based instruments will play in the Simpler sampling instrument, which has rebuilt in Live 6 specifically for this purpose, but more importantly, will play and be fully editable in the new Sampler multisampler instrument; the new Live device which will give third-party sampler designers a few sleepless nights.

Get the boxed version of Live 6 for the discs and the extras? Or save a few Euros and grab the download? Both are good – you choose!

New in the Session View

The Session View mixer has been updated – it's now resizable, and features a peak level indicator. Something needs to happen with the Arrangement mixer, too, if you ask me; I'd like the option to see the same mixer layout in either view. A new follow action, called 'other', has been added – this will lead on to playing any clip in the follow action group apart from the current one. Shift-click on multiple scenes or tracks for cut/copy/paste/duplicate/delete. It's very useful to be able to duplicate an entire track!

New in the Arrangement View

In the Arrangement View, Warp markers can now be set across multiple audio tracks – good news for producers and remixers, or anybody else working with many linear audio tracks. Also, because it's possible to multi-select clips in Arrangement tracks, they can be shortened/lengthened as one. QuickTime movies can now be dropped into the timeline to create video clips. Any locator can be nominated as the song start position. Arrangement audio clips have an extra clip view switch – Slave/Master; all clips default to the Slave setting, but if you nominate a clip as Master, then the clip plays at its original tempo, and the rest of the set syncs to it. If you create several Master clips, the lowest one will override the others. An addition to the device chooser - 'Show Automated Parameters Only – lets you choose to view only the device or mixer parameters which have had automation applied.

Clips

Command/ctrl-drag in a MIDI clip's velocity editor, and you can draw a line which any highlighted velocity markers will conform to. Use the context menu to crop samples... bringing a much-requested audio editing feature within the Live interface.

Routing

When routing audio between tracks, you can choose to take the audio from different points. Pre FX takes the audio from the source track before it's passed through any loaded effects, and before the mixer (so the pan/volume settings will be ignored). Post FX takes the audio after it's passed through any loaded effects, but before the mixer. Post Mixer takes audio from after

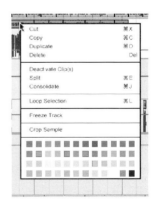

Live's Context menu

Live's pre/post/fx-mixer options

the mixer stage. If you're taking audio from a track that contains multiple device racks, you'll see Pre FX, Post FX, and Post Mixer options available for each chain in the rack.

Hardware control/MIDI/keyboard mapping

Enter MIDI Map Mode, and you can view all current MIDI mapping assignments in the Browser – very useful. This is also the place to go if you want to edit minimum/maximum MIDI values accessible by a particular controller. It's also now possible to assign multiple destinations to MIDI or computer keyboard 'qwerty' controls – so one knob, fader, or letter can affect several parameters at the same time. Instant mapping support for many popular hardware controllers reduces set-up time.

Miscellaneous

When dragging a clip between Session and Arrangement views – no need to click and (slightly) move it before hitting tab. Just click and hold on the clip, hit tab, and you're in the other view. Control click on a device and choose to lock it to a particular MIDI hardware controller (up to 6 can be used at one time). Many more clip colours are now available. Extra feedback from boxes showing numeric values – an orange 'progress bar' shows the value from left to right.

There's more, of course… but this gives you an idea of what to expect, and many of these will be appearing throughout the book, as I said at the top of this chapter. If we run across any that I didn't mention here, well… just look out for them!

Get organised

Don't panic – I'll keep the 'sensible' stuff to a minimum; you've probably got a computer and installed Live already, so let's skim through that quickly and get on to some need-to-know stuff – the necessities of Live Life, the things that have to be done before you can start rockin; a little learning, a little housekeeping, some practical stuff, some organisation – how to collate the many samples and presets that you've generated, and Ten Top Transitional Tips for people coming to Live from other sequencers such as Cubase, GarageBand, Logic – and previous versions of Live.

First things – very first things...

Installation
Downloading, purchasing, and registering Live is all covered perfectly well in the Ableton manual, and on their website; it's really quite simple, and I have no interesting anecdotes to add on these subjects...sorry.

Mac or PC?
To answer a question with a question – does it matter? In many ways, Macs and PCs are running pretty equal these days. It takes more than the biggest GHz to make the best computer platform – I believe that ease of use and reliability are more important, and in these respects OSX remains far superior to Windows.

System requirements
These are the recommended system requirements for Live 6: Mac: G3 or faster (G5 or Intel recommended), 512 MB RAM, OSX 10.2.8 or later. Windows: 1.5GHz CPU or faster, 512 MB RAM, Windows 2000/XP, Quicktime 6.4, compatible soundcard. For any music purposes, the faster your computer, the more RAM you have, and the bigger your drive, the better! If you haven't maxed out your RAM yet, please do so as soon as possible.

Check for updates
Take frequent trips to the Ableton website to ensure you have the very latest version. Ableton are refreshingly honest about posting bug fixes, and their updates are always worth having.

Cracks
Yes, there are illegally 'cracked' copies of Live floating around the internet –

Live's check for updates menu item

see my earlier comments about this. If nothing else, be warned that they don't work very well, and those who use cracked copies of Live eventually admit defeat and pay for the real thing.

Another use for Demo Mode
If you're taking Live onstage, burn a CD containing the Live installer and your final Live set. If your computer develops any problems, install Live on another computer, and run it in Demo Mode for the gig (it's probably best not to have any third-party effects or instruments in your set, unless you can easily install them on a 'strange' computer too).

Managing your computer's resources
The things that most affect your computer's ability to deal with Live are decided when you buy it. Factors like clock speed (in MHz or GHz) and system bus bandwidth (how much data can flow through at one time), and drive speed (in RPM) all affect performance. The general computer 'tips' apply – it's just stating the obvious, like shut down any unnecessary applications or processes; the less your computer has to do at one time, the happier it'll be; more screen space is useful; more money will buy you more tracks and more simultaneously effects.

There are many ways to reduce CPU usage in Live. Turn off anything in Live that isn't necessary, especially effects that aren't in use. Disable any unused mono or stereo audio inputs, and put effects on return tracks. If you're working with instruments such as Impulse or Operator, turn off any unused LFOs or filters, and reduce the number of voices available – this goes for third-party instruments too. Avoid the 'spread' function in Operator and Simpler. Turn off any unused function in Sampler. Avoid the Reverb's 'First Class' Global setting. Be discriminating with the Hi-Q clip option, use mono samples wherever possible, and trim off unwanted parts of audio clips. You'll be amazed at how small a complete Live set can be. If you render any MIDI instrument clips, and unusual effects, to audio clips, your set will also run more easily during performances – and don't forget track freeze. This has been improved to allow most regular Live functions to be applied to frozen tracks – editing, automation, etc.

Frozen tracks can also be flattened into new audio clips. Residing in the Edit menu, Flatten will replace a MIDI track or audio track containing automation or devices with an audio file representing the finished result, as if it has been resampled from the master output. All devices contained within the original track will disappear, so if you want to be able to return to them later, duplicate the track before flattening it, and then deactivate the non-flattened track.

Info – Making a noise – or not

A very common error with my students – if you suddenly lose your Live audio out, make sure that you haven't got any effects like Gate, EQ3, or Auto Filter, on extreme settings that will totally silence a track (or the entire set if they're on the master track)...also look out for any Arrangement View automation that you may have forgotten about, such as fade outs...oops!

What hardware do you need?

At the lowest level, you need headphones and audio cables to run Live – nothing else, it's all USB candy and FireWire treats. That's the Zen way. In reality, the world is full of fun stuff to give you more 'hands-on' control, and better quality audio in/out (with more channels). Work with Live on its own for a while, before spending money on extras – your ideas about 'ideal' accessories will evolve quickly.

Signal routing, ins and outs

When it comes to routing audio and MIDI, Live gives you the best of all possible worlds; the concepts are simple to understand, but the potential is there to create powerful set-ups. Audio from a particular track can go to the send/return channels, the master output, the cue output for pre listening, and to any other audio track in your Live set, including multiple tracks simultaneously. It's the same story with MIDI – send MIDI to several tracks with different audio instruments simultaneously, combine several MIDI tracks into one, send/receive MIDI to/from external software and hardware. A good starting point is to set your inputs to either 'no input' or 'external in', and your outputs to 'master', and then change them as necessary. I/O is another suspect if you're getting Live Set Silence – keep an eye on your ins and outs!

Do the Lessons

Live includes great Lessons, available via View/Lessons. Study them all, even if at first glance they don't seem relevant to you; the Operator tutorials are

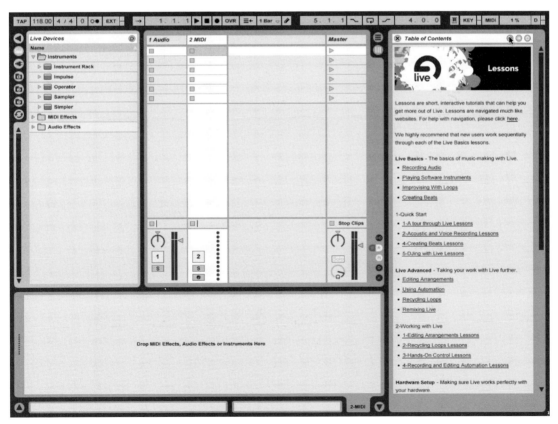

Live lessons

Live Context menu for library

particularly useful, if you're having trouble figuring out what that enigmatic interface is about!

Shortcuts

Live has always been great for keyboard shortcuts – see the full list in the Live manual; you'll have favourite shortcuts already, but there's probably others you'd use, if only you remembered them. There's also the context menu, which includes items only available via shortcuts. You can try the context menu on any part of Live's interface – right-click (PC) or ctrl-click (Mac) – and see what pops up; for example the context menu will show quite different things in the Browser (search in folder, create folder, analyze audio, are a few) or in the MIDI Editor (Adaptive Grid, Fixed Grid, Draw Mode). See my top ten keyboard shortcuts at the back of this book.

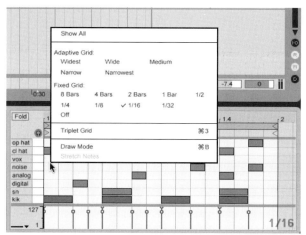

Live Context menu for MIDI clip editor

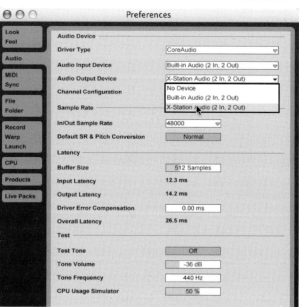

Audio output preferences

> ### Info – not seeing what you think you should?
>
> If the In/Out section doesn't show the options that you think should be available, go to Preferences, and check that Live's identified your audio/MIDI hardware. Even if the hardware is listed, you still need to activate the relevant ins/outs in the list, before they're available.

Configuring with audio/MIDI hardware

In Preferences you can determine which Input and Output Audio Devices Live uses (only one of each – with a few exceptions), buffer size and latency, and sample rate. Once you've selected the relevant hardware, use the Channel Configuration buttons to choose exactly which inputs/outputs Live will use – you can set these to mono or stereo, and remember to save CPU by disabling any that you won't be using. These configurations aren't set in stone – they'll change whenever you add new hardware, or if you occasionally work without your regular set-up, using your computer's standard soundcard instead.

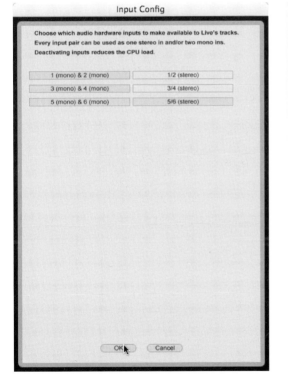
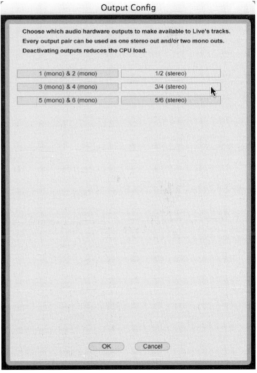

Input and Output Config panels

Managing files and sets

This admin stuff is sexy. Yes. Why? Because it'll save you heaps of time, and help you organise your source material in a logical and accessible way. It's possible to drop entire Live sets, or their elements, from the Browser, directly into a new Live set. On the same theme, the File menu includes an 'open recent Live set' item, and audio files can be dragged into Live's Session or Arrangement Views directly from your desktop; they can't be dragged out the same way though! See the next chapter for more on Live's 'Manage Files' menu item.

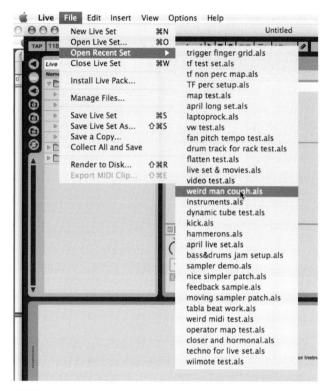

(Left) Open recent set menu item
(Right) Browsing/loading of sets

Info – a little nag-time about Collect All and Save

This File menu item is important, for backing up your files or sharing projects with other people – it copies all audio material referred to by your Live set into the project folder. See 'Managing Files & Sets' for more on this.

Collect All and Save menu item

Keeping file sizes down

In the interests of disk space, RAM, and CPU preservation, it will behove you (yes, behove) to keep your audio files small. There are various ways to do this:

- Record audio in mono when possible (use Channel Configuration/Input Config to enable this).
- Convert stereo clips to mono if stereo isn't required – do this by resampling (recording to another track), or rendering to disk

(remembering to choose Convert to Mono) and reimporting.
- Reduce the sample rates and bit rates of audio files. Live can play clips of different sample rates together quite happily.
- Once you've decided which portion of a particular clip you want to use, use an audio editor to trim the ends off. No audio editor? Well, there are other means...read about consolidation and cropping in the 'Clips And Scenes...' chapter.
- Clip RAM Mode, activated by the RAM switch in the Clip View, is used to load the currently selected audio clip into your computer's RAM; this can help take the load off your hard drive if it's struggling to read enough tracks at once. However, this obviously increases RAM usage – a trade-off.

Templates

Go to 'Preferences/File-Folder' and click on the 'Save Current Set as Template' button. Your current Live set will be saved as a template; all new Live sets you create will be based on this model – great if you have a favourite setup that you use for all your songs. A template includes all tracks, routings, MIDI and computer keyboard mappings, devices, and clips – although it won't act as a self-contained document, so if you move the audio flies referred to by your template's clips, then – too bad. It's been suggested that Live might one day save multiple templates, Logic-style, but the recent changes to the Browser and the introduction of the Library probably make this redundant.

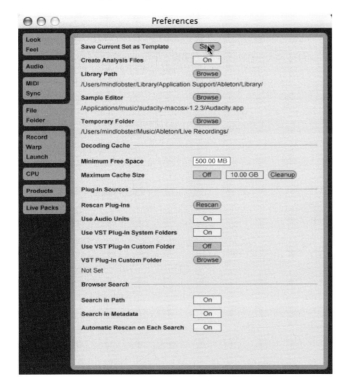

(Above) Overwrite template alert
(Left) Save template button

The Browser

The Browser has become the centre of the Live universe, and it's going to be your best friend when it comes to organisational matters. Use it to browse and load device presets, to search, browse, preview, and load audio files, and to create, rename, or delete folders. MIDI files appear as folders containing individual tracks, ready to drag into your set. Double-click a folder to make it the root for a File Browser slot. You'll find that you're always changing your default Browser folders; at the moment mine are 1) Live Library (there are other ways of jumping quickly to the Library, as I'll mention shortly), 2) current Live sets, 3) unarchived samples.

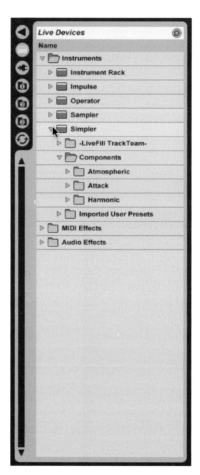 

Browsing of device presets and (right) iTunes in browser

> **Tip**
>
> iTunes is a great 'accessory' for the Live Browser – see 'Get More Sounds'.

Just as MIDI files can be cracked open in the Browser, so can Live sets. They function like folders – open a Live set 'folder' and you'll see sub-folders relating to each track, and within each track sub-folder you'll see all the clips contained within that track. These can be previewed and dragged into your current set just like any other Live Clip. The big news though, is that you can also drag the entire set into your current one; if there aren't enough tracks in the current set, new ones will be created. This enables you to easily build a new Live set using sections from previous ones – about time!

- You could go on stage with just your first song loaded, then decide the running order of your set on the fly (every technical book has to say 'on the fly', it's in the rules).
- This method could also help if you don't have enough memory to load enormous Live sets – you can just load a few songs at a time.
- Dropping in new sets is smooth – you can do it while the previous song is playing, and there won't be any dropouts.
- If you can come up with a standard format for your Live set – the same number of tracks every time, for example – then you can drop in new songs without worrying about creating extra tracks, or loading extra effects.

Info – create a standard format for Live sets

When I'm putting a new tune together, it can go lots of different ways; it's not possible to have a consistent template for that situation – varying numbers of software instruments, audio clips, MIDI envelopes, ReWiring to Logic or Reason. When I'm preparing my Live performance sets, though, I do stick to a formula. All software instruments (apart from drums) and automation are rendered to audio clips. I mix down from the original number of tracks to 6 (currently – that's always subject to review), and choose a 'generic' set of send effects that'll work in a performance situation. Finally, I map MIDI or computer keyboard remote control (or both) – depending on what hardware I aim to use for that night. By keeping the same layout every time, it's possible to have a library of 'drag'n'drop songs, ready to throw into my performance at any time.

The Library

Click the bookmark triangle in the Browser title bar, and you can shortcut directly to the Live Library. By default you'll see folders for Clips, Demo Songs, Presets, Samples, Sets, VstPresets, and Waveforms. The Clips folder contains a number of Live Clips, the Sets folder is now the default location for Live Sets, and the Waveforms folder contains a selection of waveforms suitable for use in Live's sampling devices. The default Live Library content is built from Live Packs, also covered in 'Get More Sounds'. Technically speaking, all Live device presets are now part of the Library too, which is why they're accessed via the Browser window. Use the context menu to delete items from the Library.

Within the preset list for every device, there's a folder called 'Current Project'. This is a location in which you can save any presets you create, that you want to save with the current project rather than into the main Library.

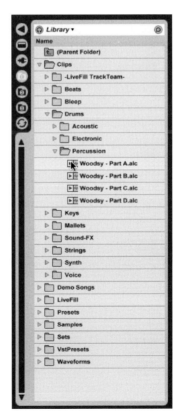

The Library

Moving to Live? Ten top transitional tips

Live isn't like other sequencers; sometimes Live isn't even like earlier versions of Live. If you're a long-term user of another sequencer, there'll be a short-ish period of adjustment...

1. Be patient. In my teaching experience, newbies have an advantage, they don't have preconceptions about where things are supposed to be or how they should work.
2. if you're used to working with beats in a certain way, or time stretching in a certain way. forget it. Live is flexible and real-time; nothing matches it for spontaneous manipulation of audio.
3. Understand the relationship between the Session and Arrangement Views; this is critical to getting the most out of Live.
4. There are some things that Live won't do, and that's where ReWire comes in handy, so you can get the best out of your 'old-world' sequencer and Live.
5. Look at Live with wide open eyes – the routing, the devices, the preferences; the solutions to many problems are right there.
6. The multi-clip assignments are real time-savers.
7. Work that browser hard – with a search function, the ability to rename items, and dragndrop creation of a library of sounds. All device preset browsing happens here now.
8. Your homework is to do the Live Lessons – this is time well spent; the best possible introduction to the Live world view.
9. Remind yourself that Live can open AIFs, WAVs, FLAC, Ogg FLAC, Ogg Vorbis, and MP3 files.
10. Live enables mapping for many extra computer keys – exactly how many depends on your keyboard, I guess!! All numerical keys, and symbols such as / or [can be used – and their upper case counterparts too.

Managing files and sets

Organising files and source material within Live has taken huge leaps. We have not one but two browsers – one on each side of the screen – and we can manage files, samples, presets, projects – everything, basically, from within Live itself, down to creating folders, and copying, moving and deleting items. This organisational stuff is at least as important as any sampling or editing innovations that have been introduced. Although this sets us up pretty well for keeping the place tidy, it takes some getting used to.

Load sets or parts of sets into another set

You don't have to reinvent the wheel – you can build a new Live set by browsing through, and then importing, previous Live sets, or parts of them – from entire tracks, down to individual clips and samples. Try it – use Live's File Browser to navigate to another Live set, and click on the small triangle at the left of the Live set's icon. As it unfolds, each track in the Live set is listed by the name you gave them. A further triangle appears next to each of these tracks. Click that to see a list of every audio or MIDI clip used in that track.

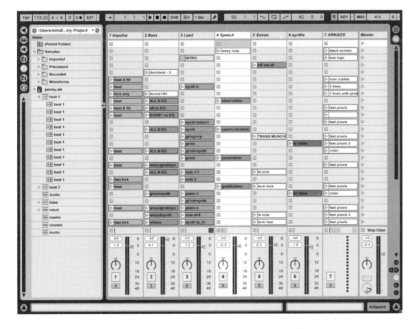

One Live set being browsed before loading into the other

If you drag in a track or clip that requires a particular effect or instrument, it will be loaded too, with the relevant preset.

See the previous chapter to read about track freezing and flattening.

Collect all and save

Live features an item in the File menu called Collect All and Save. The name says it all, really. Use this to gather together all audio material used in your Live set, including the individual samples contained within Live's sample-based instruments. This is the most immediate way to archive your Live set, for backup, or to move to another computer.

What lurks in the project folder?

After you've collected and saved, look inside your Live project folder. You'll see a new sub-folder has been created, called Samples. This contains copies of all audio files/samples referred to by your Live set. There will be more sub-folders within that one; how these are organised will depend on where your audio samples came from, and what you've done to them. For example, if you've used Impulse on a MIDI track, all sounds in your Impulse kit will appear in a folder called Drums (and even that is divided into smaller classifications, such as Cymbal, Kick, and so on), and other samples will appear in folders such as 'Imported', 'Processed', and 'Recorded'. Sometimes I feel that these Live projects create too many nested folders!

Remember too, that a project folder can contain multiple Live sets, all sharing the same samples. You might use this to keep alternate mixes of a song together, for easier archiving, and to avoid unnecessary duplication of audio samples.

> **Info**
>
> As well as organising samples within Live, it's possible to physically edit them – in a way. The 'crop sample' and 'consolidate' commands – they are non-destructive, creating new audio files in your project's samples folder. ctrl-click in clip view waveform for 'Crop Sample' and 'Manage Sample File'.

Manage Files menu item

The Manage Files item in the File menu opens up a new world of sample, set, and project management. Select this item, and the File Management browser opens at the right of the Live screen, where you'd see the Lessons. Here there are links to manage all samples used by the current set, whether they're inside the project folder, or elsewhere on your computer, or they've gone missing (you can search for them). You can view a list of all samples referenced by your Live set, with a hot-swap button for each, and, importantly, an edit button for each – the edit button has been moved from it's previous position within clip view. At the project management level, you can create Live Packs, and export all project files into the Live library. It can be slightly confusing, because you'll end up looking at both browsers at once, on left and right of the screen, which doesn't feel very intuitive...maybe it would be better to go to a full-screen Management View? I try to avoid spending time in the File Management browser, as it stands.

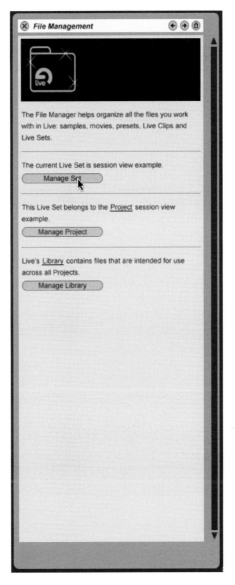

File management browser

Clips and scenes and a little on tracks

Clips and scenes are what the Session View grid is made of: clips are stacked vertically in tracks, and organised horizontally in scenes. Clips come in audio and MIDI varieties, while scenes are just – scenes. Let's start by looking at what clips have in common, rather than at the differences...

Clips in general

Clips are the building blocks of Live. Any segment of audio or MIDI that you use in Live is a clip (there's also the Live Clip format – see 'Get Organised'); a clip can even contain automation or other MIDI info, without any notes at all. Whatever type of clip you're talking about, they have common features and behaviours.

I'll assume you're mostly familiar with what clips are, and how they work; that leaves us free to look at the more interesting clip qualities, beginning with the shared attributes of audio and MIDI clips.

Clip start and end markers can be separated from the length of a clip's loop, so a clip can start playing one-shot style, then 'run into' a loop (this can also be applied to sample playback with Sampler). Whenever that clip is triggered, it will begin playing from the start marker rather than the loop start position. There are 'set' buttons for loop position, length, and clip start and end markers – these buttons are MIDI assignable, so you can go quite deep into loop manipulation from a keyboard or hardware controller.

Nudge

The Nudge buttons allow you to jump through a playing clip in increments the size of the global quantization period. Nudging can be mapped to MIDI or computer keyboard control – forwards, backwards, revert (dumps nudge offset), and keep (moves Clip Start Marker to current offset position). An extra control can be MIDI mapped – Clip Scrub Control; assign a continuous controller knob to this for free scrolling backwards and forwards. Nudge mapping is global, not clip-dependent: you don't have to assign separate controllers for every clip you want to nudge.

> **Tip**
>
> Use cmd-r on a clip to rename it without entering the clip edit view, and arrow-up/down to the next one to name that too!

Renaming a clip

Nudge controls

25

Nudge controls with MIDI mapping

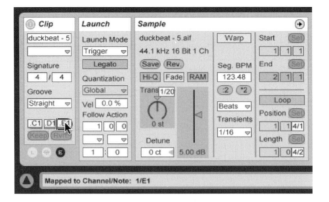

A 'nudged' clip – the dot indicating nudge offset

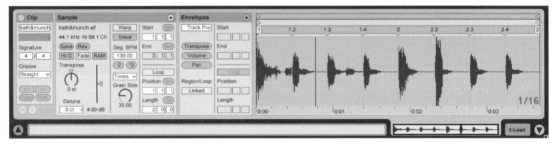

Groove

If you're used to working with MIDI sequencing, you'll be familiar with the concept of 'groove' – an attempt to humanise MIDI programming, this introduces slight offsets to note timing, just as a real instrumentalist might play a little off the beat. With Live (as of Live 4) you can apply groove settings to audio clips as well as MIDI clips – every clip has a Groove menu in the Clip View. The important thing to remember is that you have to set a Global Groove Amount in Live's control bar for clip groove to take effect.

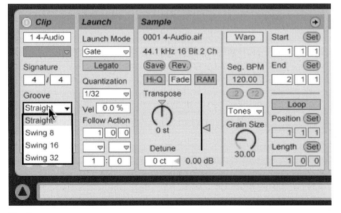

The clip groove popup menu

The global groove option

Unlinking clip envelopes

Clip envelopes – clip-level automation instructions – are effective enough, but Live has the ability to unlink envelopes from their 'host' clips; to set different loop lengths for the envelope than for the actual audio or MIDI note content. This means that clip automation envelopes can be longer or shorter than the actual clip they're attached to, giving the potential for some interesting creative effects and workrounds. You could use this technique to make a short clip fade in or out over a longer time, or to create changes to effects parameters, ie filter sweeps.

- What I most like about this is that different envelopes on the same clip can be linked or unlinked independently, and have different lengths assigned to them. In the screenshots I've got a 2-beat audio clip looping, with a 2-bar transposition envelope, and a 1-bar volume envelope. Sounds nice, and more complex than it actually is!

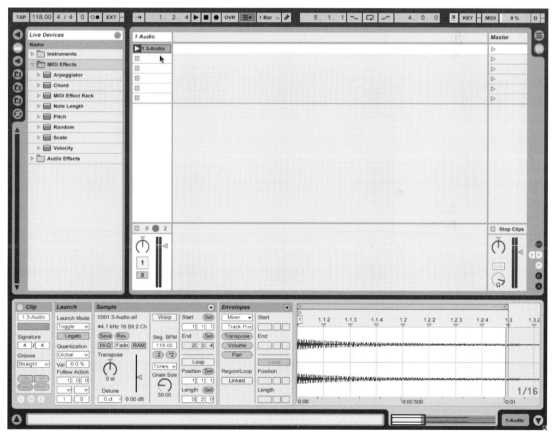

The audio clip

- If you want to seriously break the relationships between clips and their envelopes, you could turn off grid snapping, so you can draw in envelopes that don't conform to the nearest 'proper' subdivision of a bar/beat.

The unlinked transposition

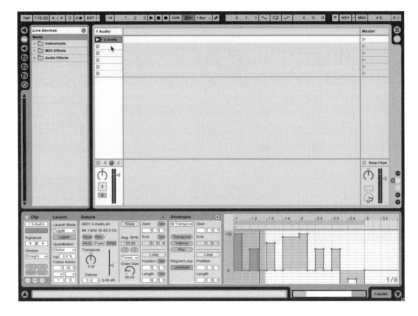

The unlinked volume

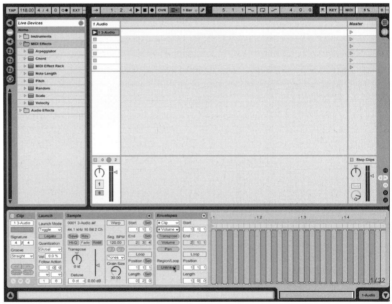

- Don't get confused – remember you have to select 'Unlinked' for every individual envelope that you want to work with.

Some of the housekeeping clip things are incredibly useful – see 'Performance Notes' for some talk about colour-coding and naming clips. Multiple clip selection is a great time-saver: shift-click on any number of clips, and you can play with the parameters remaining in the Clip View; transpose, and so on. Try it with audio and MIDI clips, and you'll get a different selection of parameters...to use the same example, transposition will no longer be available, because you can't transpose MIDI clips.

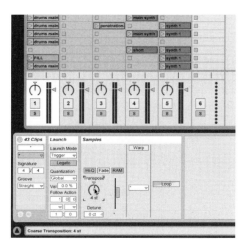

Transposition of multiple audio clips

Consolidation

If you've been bugging Ableton for an audio editor just because you want to trim clips, then leave them alone; there are a couple of ways. Got an Arrangement View clip you want to trim? Drag the edges of the clip until it plays just the piece of audio you want to hear. Zoom in to get a higher editing resolution if necessary. Use cmd-j or 'Edit/Consolidate', a short progress bar will appear, and a new audio file will be created, containing only the chosen chunk of the original. Does that count as editing? Think so. It's a philosophical thing – if you're used to working with audio editors, then you need to adjust to this way of doing things.

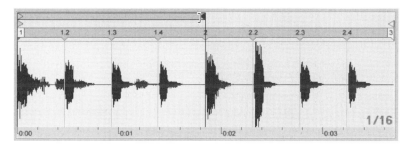

Use of loop bracket to select desired part of audio clip

- Clips must be in Arrangement View for consolidation. For clips in Session View, click-hold on the clip, hit tab, then drop it into the Arrangement View. Consolidate it, then click-hold-tab it back into Session.
- Consolidation takes place before Live's effects stage, so they're not rendered with the clip. However, any warping, gain, or transposition changes are incorporated.
- Remember you can also split clips in the Arrangement View.
- Create a more 'editor-like' appearance in Live by dragging a Live track taller, and zooming in for a closer look.
- Consolidate won't create an audio clip from a MIDI clip, although you can consolidate a MIDI clip to create another. To create an audio clip from a MIDI clip, solo the track it's on, select the MIDI clip, and render to disk, or record the MIDI clip's output to an audio track.

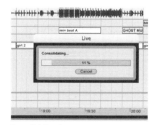

Consolidation in progress

Taller track view

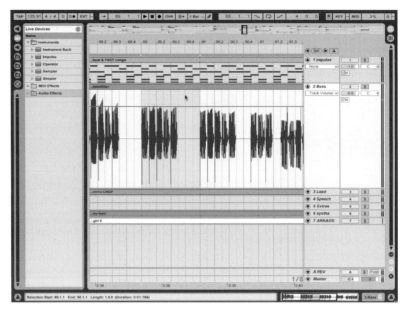

Crop sample
If you've used the clip start/end markers or loop bracket to define a portion of an audio clip, you can use 'crop sample' from the context menu to trim away the excess material on either side of the defined area. Combine this with consolidation, and you ARE editing in Live.

Clip deactivation button

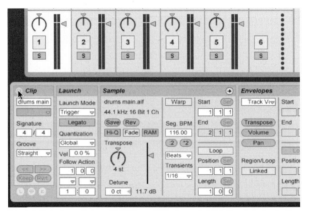

If you've got a clip or clips you want to deactivate temporarily, for some reason, there's a button just for you, next to the word 'Clip' in the Clip View window. You can also deactivate clips from the main menu or context menu.

Follow actions rule!
Follow actions do rule, it's true. While the idea of a set of clips that randomly trigger themselves may seem like you're letting the software do the talking, nothing could be further from the truth. There are so many ways to set up follow actions, so many things you can do with them, that you always feel in control. Sure, if you want to just do robot music you can, but it's your

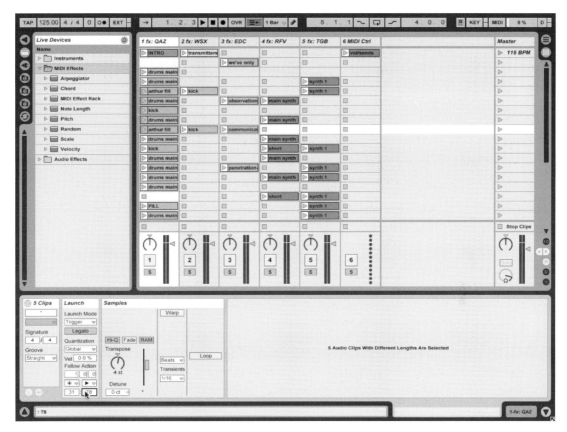

Multiple clip assignments of follow actions

choice. If you haven't explored follow actions yet, you should try them now; they're hours of fun – again, that game-like quality appears.

- You can use Live's ability to select multiple clips to assign follow action behaviours to blocks of clips at once.
- Follow actions will be included in any recording that you do, just as if you triggered each clip yourself.
- Create hundreds of short (less than a bar, but not all the same length) clips, spread them across three or four tracks, and have parallel streams of follow actions, crossing over each other at unpredictable points. Throw in some delay too – things can get quite hypnotic.
- Use follow actions to provide some unpredictable changes in your beats when jamming along with an instrument.
- Use follow actions to perform 'utility' tasks in your live sets, like maybe at the end of a song, where you have one long clip which fades over 8 bars, and you have other shorter clips which you want to stop on cue, sometime during that 8 bars.
- Follow actions are a key part of the process described in 'Live Talks To Itself!'. Thanks to ReWire (and the IAC Bus for OSX users, and – hopefully – MIDI Yoke for Windows users), you can do crazy stuff with MIDI clips and follow actions.

Live clips

Live Clips can be MIDI or audio clips, but they're not the same as plain old Session View clips; they're a way of saving clips for use in future projects, independent of the Live set they originated in. To create, one, just drag it from Session View to the Browser, and – if you like – rename it. This saves the original clip, plus all clip and envelope settings, and any devices used in the original track. If you're working on a new (empty) Live track, dragging in a Live Clip will add the necessary devices. If you're working on a track that already includes devices or other clips, then the devices won't be loaded.

Live Clips don't contain a copy of the original sample file – you could create a ton of Live Clips based on one audio clip.

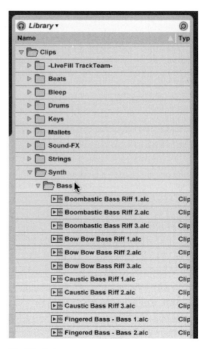

Live Clips in browser

Audio clips

When Live began, audio clips were all it had. They've come a little way since then (not a long way, because they were pretty much right first time). Many of the points to make about audio clips relate to other things mentioned in this book – every chapter has something that's relevant to audio clips, so I'm not going to repeat it all here.

Live 5 introduced the Complex warp mode; which is especially useful now that people (people in this case = DJs) are likely to be dragging entire songs into their Live sets. Complex warp mode accommodates mixed source material, so if you're using a drum loop you'd use Beats, for a keyboard part you'd use Tones, and for a song or part of a song comprising drums, bass, keyboards, guitar, and vocals, you'd use Complex.

Auto-warping is a huge time-saver – long clips are automatically warped as they're imported; from what I've seen so far Live does a good job of identifying and calculating these – especially for more straight-ahead music, you'll probably find that Auto-Warp gets it right first time. If not of course, you can still edit the markers yourself. You can also pre-warp songs/long clips by choosing 'Analyze' in the File Browser context menu. That way the song will be available for play as soon as you drop it into a Live set (otherwise it takes a little while for songs be available while they're being auto-warped). If you don't want auto warping to take place, you can disable it in Preferences/Defaults.

It's possible to add warp markers to clips while they're playing.

Live's metronome is very useful as a clinical no-doubt-about-it arbiter of time when you're working with a loop and its start/end points or warp markers. Click on the symbol in the control bar. Use the Cue Volume control to change the metronome volume.

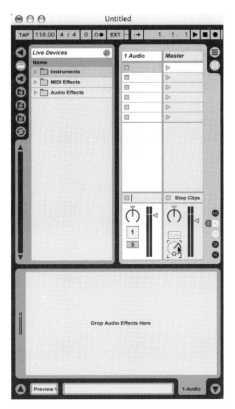

The metronome

- Shift-click on several warp markers to move them at once, retaining their relative spacing.
- You can divide and trim audio clips in Live, it's just not done in the usual way. Read about consolidation and cropping, above.
- A little reminder: there's a small Save button in Clip View, which attaches the current clip settings to the relevant audio sample (as part of the .asd file). Whenever you use this clip again in a Live set, the same settings will be applied.

Metronome volume control

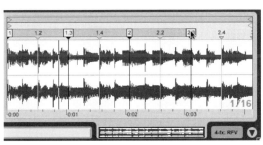
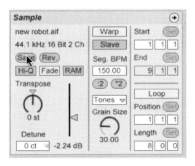

Multiple warp markers selected and (right) The save clip button

MIDI clips

I love working with Live's MIDI clips – they do such a good job of integrating MIDI with audio, it's totally fluid. If you're coming at it from MIDI hardware grooveboxes, you won't have any trouble relating to it. If you're coming from Pro Tools or Logic, it may take you a bit longer, but the differences are all good! How you create MIDI clips is up to you. I'm not a keyboard player, and after years of working with MIDI sequencers, I find Live is so comfortable to use that I'm happy to just draw in notes with the pencil tool; it doesn't get in my way at all.

However, if you do like to enter notes in real-time, then Live has some useful quantization tools. Select record quantization in the edit menu, and choose from a list of options ranging from no quantization, through eighth-note quantization, to sixteenth-note and triplets quantization. Any real-time MIDI note recording you make after this change will reflect this value, until you change it again.

'Record quantization' menu item

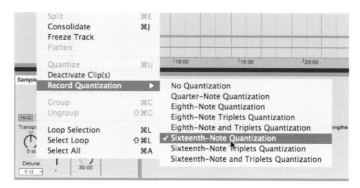

You can also apply quantization to recorded MIDI notes after the event, by selecting the note or notes and choosing quantize from the edit menu, forcing them to conform to your previously selected value, or use ctrl-u/cmd u to bring up a dialog box with more detailed quantize options, such as the resolution, adjust note start/end, and amount – the amount setting is quite useful if you want to retain any human feel to what you've recorded; instead of rigidly applying strict quantization to get a robotic feel, it'll apply the rules to a selected percentage, which can help retain some organic qualities.

The MIDI note quantization menu

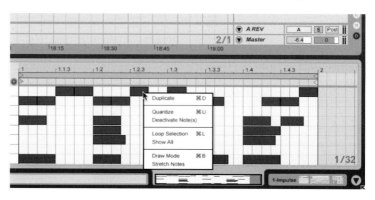

Use the context menu to view a list of resolution options for the MIDI clip grid, based upon two types of grid – adaptive (display varies according to level of zoom), and fixed (divisions remain constant).

- You can't click to create a MIDI 'clip' in the Arrangement View (like you can in Session View), but you can drag to highlight an area, then choose insert midi clip from the menu, or shift cmd m.

'Insert MIDI clip' menu item

There's also the Preview switch in the MIDI Editor, another addition that is common to DAWs – whenever you enter, or click on, or move, a note in a MIDI clip, you can hear it too.

You can use the context menu to deactivate notes within a MIDI clip. If for some reason you want to temporarily 'kill' a couple of notes within a clip, this is the way to do it. I sometimes use this when I'm creating variations on an existing MIDI part. I'll copy the clip, then deactivate the portion that I want to change. That way I can draw in the new notes while keeping the original part as a visual reference.

As well as creating MIDI parts from scratch, Live can import MIDI files created elsewhere (the internet is full of them). A MIDI file appears as a folder in the File Browser; each track within the MIDI file appears separately inside the folder; just drag them into Live as usual.

- You can preview MIDI clips in the File Browser, just like audio clips – you'll hear them with the correct instrument sound, even if you haven't loaded the instrument into your Live set yet.

Exporting MIDI from Live isn't so tidy – you can only export individual MIDI clips, there's no way to save a type 0 or type 1 MIDI file containing all the MIDI tracks in your set. I guess if you've built a lot of MIDI tracks in the Arrangement View, you could export them individually and re-assemble in another sequencer. Looped MIDI clips will only export as one-shots – although you could consolidate them first. The other way to do it would be to send MIDI via ReWire to another sequencer, like Reason, and record it in real-time. Doing anything like that in real-time seems ugly these days, but it's better than nothing!

Scenes

When you want to trigger a bunch of clips simultaneously, you put them in a horizontal row and trigger that from the right-hand (master) track. These rows are called scenes. You can construct a Live set in Session View, and spend your performance simply clicking your way vertically through the scenes. If this is all you do, it's pretty low-maintenance; maybe a bit too easy. But if you use this as the basis of your set and add some one-shots, effects control, some freewheeling unstructured sections – why not?

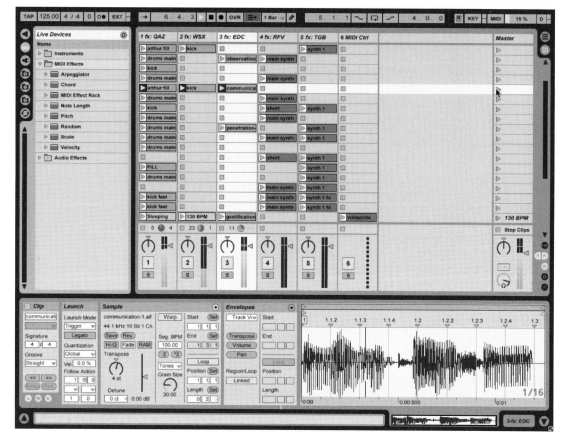

A scene-highlighted horizontal row

There are several different ways to trigger scenes. You got your basic clicking, but you can also assign a MIDI note or a character from your computer keyboard (you can trigger scenes via MIDI clips if you read 'Live Talks To Itself!'). When you enter Key Map Mode or MIDI Map Mode, scene-specific controls appear at the bottom of the Master track – Scene Launch, Scene Up, Scene Down, and Scene Select (scrolling). I use the transport controls on the Ozonic to work with these; they'd also be great if you're playing an instrument, you could use something like Behringer's FCB1010 foot controller to scroll up and down through scenes.

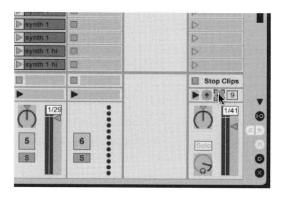

Scene select MIDI assignments

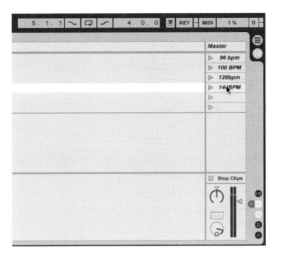

Scene bpm

Scenes can be used to trigger BPM changes, a feature which, when introduced, made a world of difference to performing with Live. All you have to do is name the clip something like '96 BPM'. You can type it in different ways: 96 bpm, 96 BPM, 96bpm, or 96BPM – they all work; BPM 96 doesn't work!

- If you've got a lot of scenes to name, do it fast: rename the first one as usual, then use the tab key to move on to the next.

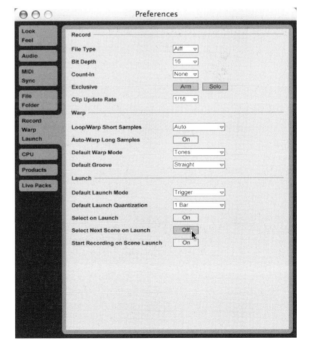

'Select next scene on launch' preferences item

Scenes can be copied, pasted, deleted, and duplicated, like anything else. They have some other interesting characteristics: in Preferences, you can choose 'Select Next Scene on Launch', which enables you to move downwards through scenes just by pressing 'enter' or 'return'. If you choose 'Start Recording On Scene Launch', any armed clips in the launched scene will start recording.

- Capture And Insert Scene is one that I always try to remember. It copies all playing clips in the current scene into a new one immediately below, very handy for when you're working on song structures.

In case you're wondering, you can't save scenes with BPM info to the Library, as such. You can drag a row of clips in the Browser, and they'll be saved, but it doesn't save the scene name or BPM settings. You could create a Live set containing just the BPM scene, and drag that into the

Browser, then drag that back into whatever set you want to use it in. I can't see any use for this at the moment, but maybe something will come up!

Scenes are an essential part of using Live's Session View – they relate equally to live performance and songwriting.

'Capture and insert scene' MIDI item

Song header scenes

In 'Performance Notes' I describe how to build a Live set that contains several songs, arranged vertically in the Session View, and I talk about the importance of labelling and colour coding. Another useful thing is to create a header that divides the songs (visually), and makes room for some useful labelling – a line drawn across the Live set, with the song name, and any other info that might be useful, like reminders of BPM or channel changes.

The first thing you have to do is create a silent audio clip. You can do this by creating and arming an empty audio track, selecting another track (where nothing's playing) as an audio source, and hitting record, then trimming the resulting clip to 1 bar in length. Then copy it, colour it, and label it as necessary – see my screen shots; I use yellow for my headers.

- These don't send any MIDI info or play any sounds; they're just visual guides.

Routing audio between tracks

Here's that little bit on tracks promised in the chapter title…

Sending audio to return tracks

For every Return track that you create – ctrl-alt-t (PC), cmd-alt-t (Mac) – Live adds a Send knob to the relevant track. If you've got a Return track with an audio effect on it, you can share that effect over several tracks – very CPU efficient. It's usually best to set the effect's dry/wet control all the way to wet, using the track's Send knob to control the amount of effect. Return tracks have no Input slots, but they do have Outputs – their output can be re-routed to other tracks rather than directly to the Master track.

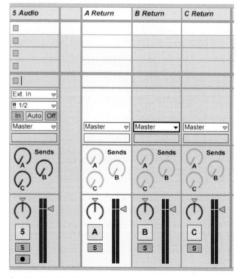

Send knobs and return tracks

Audio from one track to many

You can send the audio output from one track to several others simultaneously (this includes the audio from MIDI tracks that have instruments assigned). You could put different effects on every track, pan them differently, send some to a return track, mess with their volumes, put a Gate or EQ on them – and of course record it all. Just select the 'source' track in the Input Type slot for each 'target' track.

This feature is built into the Impulse drum sampler – you can choose each separate Impulse slot as an input source for other audio tracks.

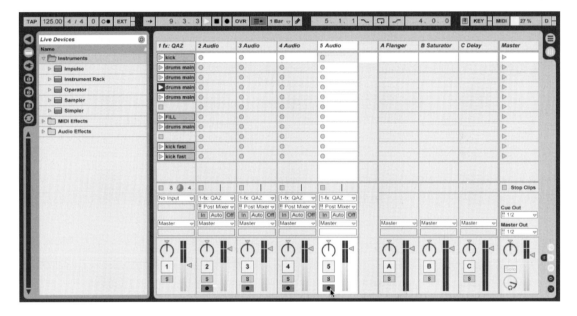

Audio routed from one track to many

- Remember to arm the track to hear the incoming audio.
- Don't get confused between recording audio or MIDI and automation; audio won't be recorded to your drive until you hit the record button in a clip slot on each track.
- This kind of routing also works with audio from an external source, like a microphone or Reason.
- You could begin a performance with an empty set, record a short piece of audio, then have fun routing it around various tracks, sends, and effects.

Audio from many tracks to one

Turn that on its head, and send the audio from several tracks to one. This is a way of re-sampling Live's output, or part of it, at any time, to further manipulate within the song. Choose the 'target' track in the Output Type slot for each 'source' track.

- Combine the two approaches: send one track to many, and simultaneously route some of the 'many' back to another single track.
- If you're recording from outside sources and have live microphones

involved, watch out for feedback – remember the monitor In/Auto/Off options.
- Create a sub mix, pre-mixing selected tracks to one, before sending it to the Master output. This lets you put the fader and pan and effect settings for several tracks at the disposal of one control for each function.

If you want to bounce everything from Live's master output to a new audio clip, select 'resampling' as the source for a new audio track's input. The output from all tracks will be routed to this new track, including effects on sends and on the master track itself. There's no danger of feedback problems, when resampling is selected, monitoring is disabled.

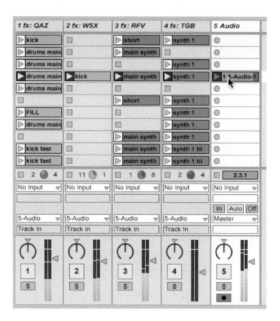

Audio routed from many tracks to one

It works with MIDI too – from one track to many

Create a MIDI clip in a new track, with some notes and/or controllers – don't add any instruments to the track. That way you'll see MIDI outputs instead of audio outputs at the bottom, and you can send those MIDI notes all over the place. Choose your 'source' MIDI track as the Input Type for each 'target' track, and arm them for recording, then add your chosen software instruments/MIDI effects for each track.

- Send the same MIDI part to two or three different instruments at once to layer sounds.
- You can also send MIDI controllers.
- Check your channel numbers. A single track can only send MIDI on one channel at a time!

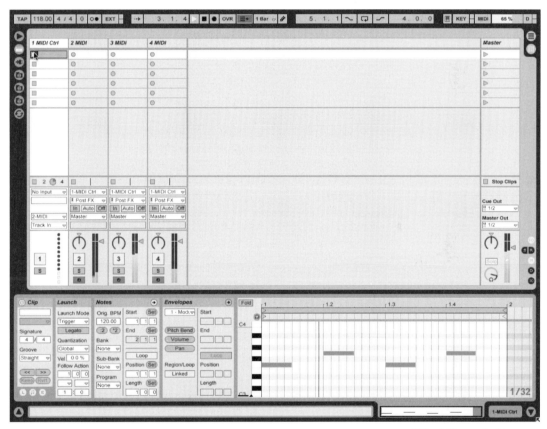

MIDI routed from one track to many

Sending MIDI from many tracks to one

And again...choose the 'target' MIDI track in the Output Type slot for each 'source' track, and arm the 'target' for recording.

- Remember not to add software instruments to the 'source' tracks, or they'll default to sending audio instead of MIDI.
- Create percussion parts with a separate track for each percussion instrument, then send them all to Impulse on the 'target' track.

MIDI routed from many tracks to one

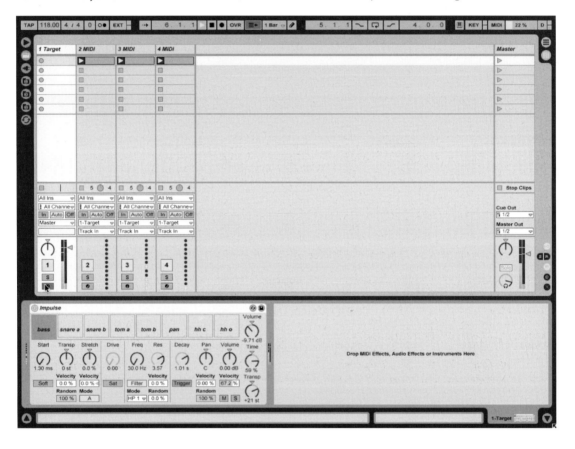

- You can bounce multiple MIDI tracks to a new single MIDI track, just like with audio. You don't need any instruments assigned to any of the tracks. This is a good way to create a new instrument part from others – I've done this before, combining two different bass parts; on a song of my own, and on somebody else's during a remix.

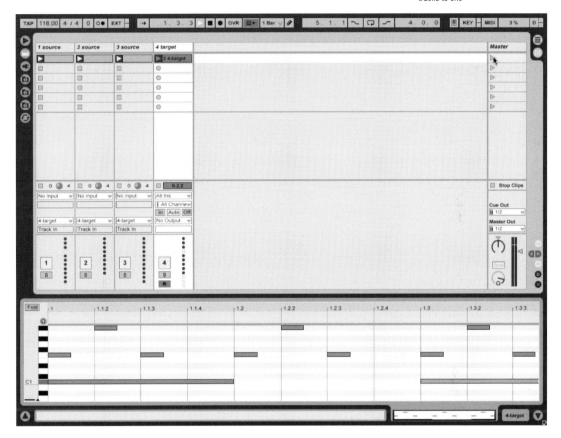

Showing MIDI bounced from many tracks to one

Devices

Live's 'native' plug-ins are divided into three categories: Instruments, MIDI Effects, and Audio Effects. There are four Instruments (that's if you paid for the Operator and Sampler upgrades), seven MIDI Effects, and twenty-four Audio Effects. These devices can also be grouped together in Device Racks. You can use third-party Audio Units and VSTs with Live, but try to get familiar with the bundled items first. The Live Device interfaces follow the trusted Ableton principles – very functional, and generally clear; they're all mappable via MIDI or the computer keyboard, and their presets can be accessed via the ever-evolving Browser/Library.

Audio effects

Live 6 introduces two new Audio Effects, and one new MIDI Effect: Dynamic Tube, EQ Eight (really an upgrade from EQ Four), and Note Length.

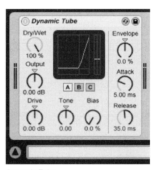

Dynamic Tube

Dynamic Tube is a distortion effect, but unlike Saturator it's designed to give a more tube-like (hence the name) quality – emulating the characteristics of typical tube amplification. Three tube models are included, each with their own variation of the typical tube performance. Tube A is a cleaner effect, which only begins to distort when the input signal reaches a certain level, while Tube C distorts all the time....Tube B is a more moderate, in-between effect. Dynamic Tube also features an Envelope Follower, which can be used to produce some interesting effects, if you juggle it with the Bias and Drive controls. A + value on the Envelope Follower means that louder parts of the input signal are more distorted than quiet parts. A – value has the opposite effect – louder parts are cleaner. It's great with drum loops, use it to make a kick or snare really crunchy... it can really change the emphasis of a groove...as one part gains more presence over the others.

EQ Eight is fully compatible with presets from EQ Four – if you load an old Live set that used EQ Four, you won't lose any of your settings. The most interesting thing about EQ Eight is the way you can apply separate EQ to both channels of a stereo input with only one instance of EQ Eight. Use the

All of Live's devices

EQ Eight

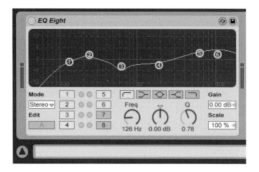

Mode button to choose L/R mode, then the Edit button below that to choose which channel you're working on. The active curve will be highlighted in the display. I love it with drum loops!

Info – overlooked plug-in of the week

Utility, in the Audio Effects folder, does some simple but handy jobs around the Live house. It has controls for mute, gain, and stereo width (right down to mono), and it also lets you invert the phase of either channel. Clicking either the L or R buttons will send the left or right channel to both outputs – use this if you have a stereo file, and you only want to process one channel.

MIDI effects

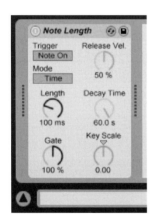

Note length

LIve 6 added the Note Length MIDI effect; this is quite like quantization in a way. You can use it with MIDI clips to force all MIDI notes to the same value, whether a determined length of time, or – in sync mode – to note values relating to your Live set's BPM. It's quite useful for changing the feel of a bass part, for example, without having to edit the notes within the clip. It's good as an effect, too, changing the length of notes on the fly from a MIDI controller or envelope. It gets really interesting when you use the Note Off mode instead of Note On; this means that we're working with the MIDI note offs instead of the usual on messages...so sounds trigger as the notes are released...this can be extremely disorientating if you're playing in from a MIDI keyboard...suddenly the notes only sound as you release the keys. One fun thing to do with this is to send your keyboard to two MIDI tracks at the same time. Let's say each track has Operator loaded, but track 2 also has Note Length, set to Note Off mode. Arm both tracks and play your keyboard. Track 2 will play notes as your release the keys on your controller, so you're getting two lots of notes, one after the other. Use Note Length to increase the duration of notes in Track 2, and add an audio effect, such as a Phaser...you'll get a nice aftertouch style effect, with a different version of the initial sound triggering as you release the keys. Add some more to it by loading Auto Pan after the Phaser, so you get a nice left-right movement as the note decays.

- You can apply any of Live's MIDI Effects to external software or hardware via ReWire, just like sending other MIDI info – just drop them into a MIDI track with some clips, but without an instrument.

Instruments

Live includes two standard Device Instruments, and two optional extras, which must be purchased separately – these extras are the Operator synth, and the Sampler multisampler. These instruments, like the Audio and MIDI Effects, have all the advantages that you'd expect from Live-native devices; huge creative potential, a consistent interface, and seamless integration into the rest of the Live universe.

The standard Instruments are Impulse and Simpler. They're variations on a theme, being alternative ways of dealing with sampling – in some ways they don't do much different from Live clips, but – as when I first started using Live to organise QuickTime loops – they repackage it more efficiently. The entire Live application itself is like a giant sampler anyway, so you can think of Impulse and Simpler as being samplers within a sampler; microcosms of what Live does on a larger scale, rather than software samplers in the vein of EXS or Halion. Dragging and dropping of samples is the key with these instruments. You can drop in a sample from the Browser, or an audio clip, or your computer desktop, and start triggering it immediately. This is almost toy-like simplicity compared to some other sampling systems, but it doesn't lack for tweaking options.

When I first looked at Impulse, I was a little confused. I'd been using Reason to create drum parts for some time, and I was expecting the slots in Impulse to somehow correspond to steps in a sequence. Once I realised that Impulse was kind of a blank sample playing instrument, and it interacted with MIDI clips like any other, then – no problem. Live's collage philosophy comes into play at instrument level too – Impulse's drag'n'drop friendliness encourages you create 'kits' that combine sounds of all types; of course you can

Impulse with eight sample slots available

save these kits in the Library for future re-use (don't forget to 'collect and and save' your set if you want to transfer it to another computer). The most fun part with Impulse is the fact that each of the eight loaded sounds can be treated totally independently. Even better, each sound can be assigned to a separate audio output, for wild routing games. See 'Clips And Scenes...' for more information on routing audio and MIDI in Live.

Quote

'I love the way the Simpler works. Just drag an audio file from anywhere (the arrangement, a folder), and drop into the plug-in, it's so simple and quick.' – *Jody Wisternoff, Way Out West*

- If you're routing one of Impulse's outputs to another audio track for effects processing, you don't need to record it as audio on that second track before you render your song – it will be included anyway, with – of course – the effects in place.

One of the few things I used Reason for was its retro style drum machine; now I use Impulse for everything – as long as I can find the kit sounds I want. Logic has a great drum machine, called Ultrabeat, and there's no reason why that can't be used with Live via ReWire, but – again – it's not nearly so intuitive; established Live users will feel far more at ease using Impulse.

Simpler – well, it lives up to the name. Drag'n'drop, just like Impulse; it's quite like working with just one of Impulse's eight sounds. It's not a monster sampler in its own right, but as part of the larger Live picture, it works great – a very easy way to grab and start using a particular sound as a sample for playing keyboards or drawing into MIDI clips. As soon as you start moving

Simpler

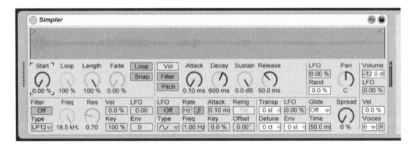

the Loop Length and Crossfade controls, your sound will begin to evolve. Follow that with some LFO assignments – apply the LFO to the filter cutoff, and to output volume.

Operator is Ableton's first synthesiser, and an optional purchase. Is it worth buying? Yes – for the quality sounds, and for the Live design continuity. You don't have to be a synth whiz to use Operator, though its interface is quite mysterious at first. I often start by calling up a preset, and editing that, rather than reinventing the wheel every time. Operator is primarily about the four oscillators at the left of the display. Each one can play a different waveform, and their levels can be mixed to create a new sound. Each oscillator affects the sound of the preceding oscillator, and the order in which this happens can be set by choosing a particular algorithm – click on the little boxes at the bottom right of the central display to view these. The volume envelope loop modes are fun, too – great for applying rhythmic structures to

Operator

your sounds...and I enjoy the Time control, a single knob which will proportionally increase or decrease all envelope time-based values within operator; for example the volume envelope loops, the LFO, and so on.

Live's Lessons give Operator thorough coverage, showing you how to create bass, percussion, lead, or pad sounds – Ableton are obviously eager to make sure we appreciate this thing. The presets do a good job of reflecting the sonic possibilities, so if necessary you can use Operator straight away, and figure out how it works later!

Sampler is a multisampler which takes Live's native sampling features to a different level, with the highlights being the import of samples from other formats such as Akai, Giga, and EXS, and an excess of signal routing options. The easiest way into Sampler is to work with a sample in Simpler first, then control-click on the Simpler title bar, and choose Simpler -> Sampler. This will replace Simpler with Sampler, retaining any loops and crossfades you've already created. Then you have a lifetime's worth of parameters to play with,

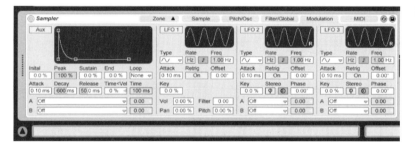

Sampler modulation tab

starting with Key and Velocity Zones, and moving on to Pitch and Oscillator Envelopes, then into total mental meltdown with a freely-assignable Auxiliary Envelope, and no less than three assignable LFOs. If the Release Loop Mode in the Sample tab doesn't appear to be doing anything, go to Filter/Global and extend the Volume Envelope's Release Time.

Device racks

In the browser, alongside the Instruments and Effects, you'll notice Device Racks. These replace the device groups in earlier versions of Live, and although the basic principle is the same – grouping together instruments and effects to create a preset combining both elements – the implementation is far more complex. Device racks can contain limitless numbers of Instruments and Effects within their MIDI-selectable chains, and there are 8 macro knobs available for MIDI mapping of multiple controls. If that isn't enough, a rack can also contain other racks.

Creating a rack is easy – select adjoining devices and choose Group from the context menu. You can separate the elements at any time by choosing Ungroup.

- Some of the preset Device Racks are quite CPU-heavy, especially those featuring multiple reverbs, so you might need to call on track freeze when working with these.
- See the 'Performance' chapter for a specific example of using device racks.

Device delay compensation

This is Live's way of dealing with the slight delay that can occur when an audio signal is input and then comes out the other end – all tracks are kept in sync, and hopefully there is little if any apparent delay between what goes in and what comes out. I've found certain latency problems have disappeared between earlier updates to Live.

If you open a pre-Live 5 set, device delay compensation defaults to off, and you'll have to activate it manually in the Options menu. Generally Ableton recommend leaving this on at all times, but if you're having severe latency problems when recording instruments, you could try turning it off.

- If you're recording an external audio source like a voice or an instrument, and running it through some of Live's audio effects, remember that it won't 'print' the effects with the performance unless you route the audio out from the track with effects to another audio track, and record it there.

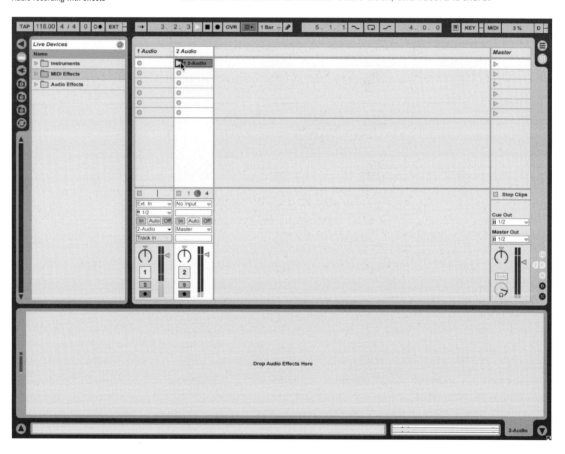

Audio recording with effects

Vintage Warmer

It may seem funny when Live is such a blatantly 'electronic' instrument, but sometimes you crave more 'human' qualities. This is reflected in several different areas of Live use, the groove quantization features being the main example. Another area where this can be a concern is in processing, where subjective 'warmth' is a desirable thing. Reason includes the M Class Mastering Suite, which trades heavily on punch, clarity, volume, and sweetness – attributes which are considered to be very desirable, and to make your song sound like a 'proper' recording. At the time of writing Live doesn't have anything like this as an integrated device (although some of the preset Device Racks venture into this territory), but there are other plug-ins that you can use. PSP AudioWare's Vintage Warmer EQ plug-in is a popular choice; this will make your Live sets sound better than spending the same amount of cash on an 'effect' plug-in, or sample CDs, or yet another 'ultimate' MIDI controller.

Vintage Warmer

Vintage Warmer contains 31 pre-sets, with something for every occasion – individual instrument tracks or entire mixes can get the treatment. It's available in VST/AU/DX formats, so it's Mac and PC compatible. You can of course save your own pre-sets. This is a guaranteed way to add those magic sprinkles to your live set – volume, punch, warmth – aaahh, yes!

Download the Vintage Warmer demo and do some A/B testing through your regular speakers. You don't have to understand the mysteries of multi-band mastering (which is good because I'd be in trouble), you can hear it working.

Sampling in Live

The term 'sampling' is in a new context now...it's just a word game. Live is at least 50% about sampling – remember that! And as a result, it's hard to isolate 'sampling' subject matter, when it permeates the entire Live experience. So we're going to arbitrarily decide that – as far as this chapter goes – 'sampling' mostly happens within Live's three sampling instruments; Simpler, Impulse, and Sampler. Mostly, that is, because we can also include the basic Live audio clip in any discussion about sampling.

Audio clips

Audio clips are audio files of any length, which can be triggered from the computer keyboard or via MIDI. They can be loops, or one-shots. They can be transposed and cropped. Need I go on? You know this already.

You can have lots of fun with a MIDI keyboard and audio clips, it's almost like a forgotten feature, in the midst of Live's other sampling adventures. You can quickly map an audio clip across any number of keys on a MIDI keyboard (sadly it doesn't work with Live's virtual computer keyboard).

Audio clip

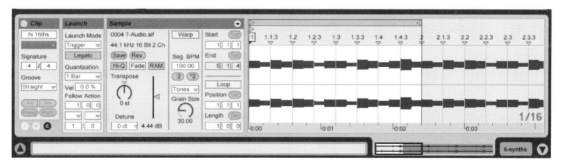

When you have a clip mapped to a MIDI note, hit apple/cmd m, and when you click on the clip, you'll get a Status Bar message saying: 'Mapped to Channel/Note: 1/C0 (or whatever) (Press multiple keys above or below this one to define a note range.)' Hold down, say C-2 and C2, and then hit cmd-m to exit midi mapping mode. Now play your keyboard within the defined range, and you'll hear that clip pitched up and down across the keys. This is a fast way of getting a sample working for you, and it saves filling your screen with multiple, differently-pitched, copies of the same clip.

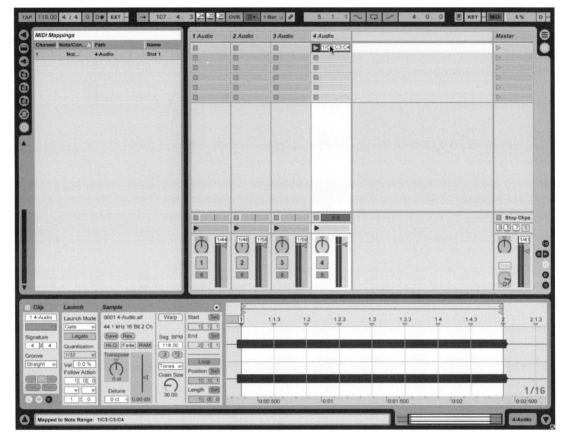

Fast MIDI mapping

You could use it to create a cruder version of an existing sound in your synth or sampler. Create an audio recording of a single C note, say 'C0'. Then assign low and high MIDI notes to it as described above, so that the sound is 'forced' to play over a range of a couple of octaves. This will undo a lot of careful work somebody has done to make something sound and behave like a 'proper' sample – so what?

This feature may seem redundant, when it's so easy to just drop a sample into Simpler, and achieve better results, but it's quick and dirty, and that's good!

Simpler

Simpler is a basic container for one sample, which adds an element of synthesis-type control to the usual sampling features such as crossovers and loop points. Drop in an audio clip, and you can quickly transform it to something else altogether. If you've got a MIDI controller with knobs to spare, map the Loop Length, Sample Length, and Loop Crossfade Amount controls for some real-time editing. Although I stated that Simpler is a container for one

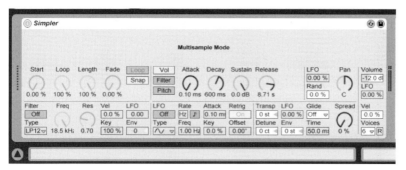

Simpler in multisample mode

sample, it also has a Multisample Mode, which enables it to play multisamples which would otherwise require the Sampler add-on product. The main difference is that Simpler gives playback only of these multisample patches – no editing is possible.

Impulse

Impulse is a drum machine or drum sampler, with 8 slots for containing sounds. You can, of course, load any type of sound into it, not just drums! Impulse has synth type parameters too, some of which are applied on a slot level, others are applied on a global level, across the entire 'instrument'. Impulse integrates with the MIDI clip view, displaying slot names vertically at

Impulse

the left, very helpful when programming drums. Record some sounds on your mobile phone and mix those up with 'cleaner' drum sounds...I have one I use which sounds great...a big nasty drum crunch recorded at a friend's gig.

Sampler

Sampler is the latest addition to Live's sampling resources. A true multisampler, capable of combining many different samples to recreate the sound of a 'real' instrument, or to produce otherwise unattainable electronic sounds. What Sampler brings in power, it also gains in complexity, but it compares well to other samplers on the market, and is a major step towards Live's credibility as a self-contained workstation. Crucially, Sampler can import from multi-gigabyte instrument libraries in popular formats such as EXS/Garageband, Akai, Gigastudio, Creative/Emu, Soundfonts, and Kontakt.

You may want to live with the Sampler demo for a while before purchasing either it or any 'rival' sampling plug-ins. Sampler is quite unusual, and clearly oriented more for synthesis and mangling than the faithful reproduction of real instruments. There are some people who use Sampler for everything, while others use it alongside other sampling applications.

It's not possible to record audio directly into Sampler, Impulse, or Simpler, as you can do with hardware samplers, and some software samplers (maybe).

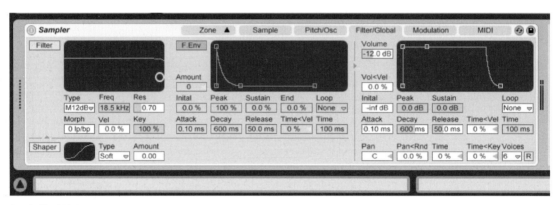

Sampler filter/global tab

But that's not really a problem; it's not necessary, given the way Live works – as I'm overly fond of saying, the entire application is a colossal sampler at heart, and Impulse/Sampler/Simpler are like mini-samplers that reside within the Great Live Sampling Entity.

Info

The hot-swap button is available in all Sampling instrument devices. It appears in each Impulse slot, in the sample display in Simpler, and in the Sample tab and sample layer list within Sampler. With this button we can replace a sample with any other sample. Click it, and you'll be taken to the file browser, where you can use your arrow keys, and 'enter', to navigate through and load samples. Hot-swapping can also be applied to device presets.

Automation

Automation is what they call it when you record changes to mixer or effects settings, so that the changes can be replayed or edited when the song is played back later. You're not 'burning' those changes into the audio of your song, the automation data (called envelopes) is recorded separately – it's non-destructive.

The 'what to click and where' aspects of automation are well-covered in the Live manual. One thing to understand about automation in Live is that it happens at both clip and track levels, and it relates to the way that you can record and play back performances.

Pretty much everything can be automated in Live, except transport commands – you can get Live to stop itself, but you can't get it to start itself again (see 'Live Talks To Itself!' for further explanation). It's easy to see which Live functions can be automated; hit cmd-m, for MIDI mapping, and any highlighted controls can be automated. Automation can be recorded in real-time, for example messages sent from a hardware controller during a performance, or it can be drawn in using Live's pencil tool. Of course, a bit of both is good – recording spontaneous movements with a hardware controller, then going through and edit them afterwards.

Clip automation in general

Exactly what you can automate at clip level depends on whether you're working with audio or MIDI clips. There are common things, however – the means by which information is entered are the same – use the pencil tool in Draw Mode, or click with the mouse to enter breakpoints, or record in real time. Any effect that's loaded in the same track as the clip can have its parameters automated, and the mixer parameters are always available – track volume, pan, and either transpose (for audio clips) or pitch bend (for MIDI clips). If you're working with a Device Rack, then the macros for that rack will also be available for automation.

- Live's clip nudge feature can also be automated – each 'nudge action' creates a new, quantized clip in the Arrangement View; see the next screen shot.

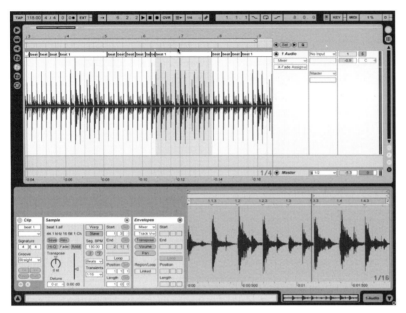

There are various ways to automate clips and tracks. If you've got any parameters assigned to hardware controllers, then start recording, move that knob or fader, and everything you do will be recorded until you hit the spacebar or stop button. Otherwise, you can 'record' your automation without even entering record. This is because – of course (newbies note) – we're not recording audio here, just the controller movements. While your clips or tracks are playing, just draw the automation in.

Separate clips created by nudge actions

MIDI clip automation

When it comes to automating MIDI clips in particular, you can automate parameters for the mixer as usual (plus send levels for any send effects), software instruments, and any audio effects in line after the instrument. If you don't have an instrument on the track, you can send MIDI controllers to other apps or hardware. You also have the option of sending MIDI Bank, Sub-bank, or Program changes.

MIDI controllers available with a MIDI clip

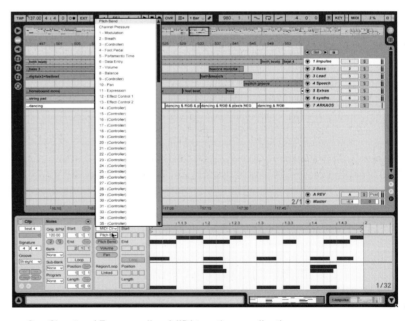

- See Chapter 15 on sending MIDI to other applications.
- Each track can only send on one MIDI channel at a time!

Audio clip automation

After a little while, you'll see how working with MIDI clips is a fragmented version of 'regular' MIDI sequencing, which has its roots in the 1980s (that's not to underestimate it, though). Audio clips are a different proposition, especially as regards clip automation – these are things that were impossible before. I'm talking about the amazing warp markers, the warp mode options, clip groove...even the transposition at clip level makes a world of difference – you can use it to really mess up drum beats, for example. Combine these features with the ability to separate automation envelopes from clip length, and you're going into unknown territory.

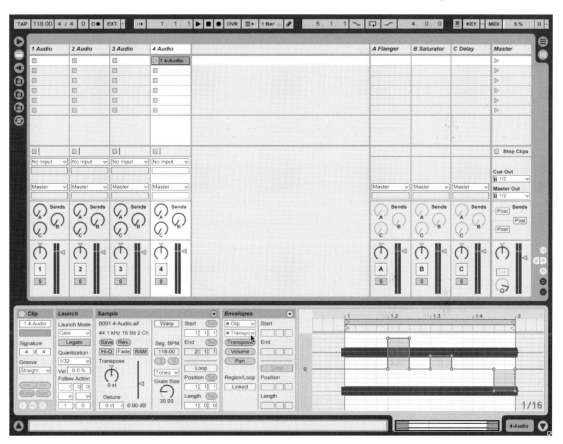

Audio clip automation

Here's an example of something I've done to an audio clip with warp markers and transposition envelopes; see the following screen shots for more reference. I took a vocal sample from an old record (name withheld to protect the innocent), and trimmed it by consolidating the clip. This wasn't a clip that needed to loop; it was going to be a one-shot. I wanted the first half of the phrase to play at normal speed, then the second half to slow down as much as physically possible. I created a warp marker at the desired point, which was conveniently the start of bar 5. I then created more warp markers and dragged them around until the end of the clip (originally coming in at 5.3) was at the end of bar 24. When triggered, this clip would play at nor-

Showing audio sample stretching in progress

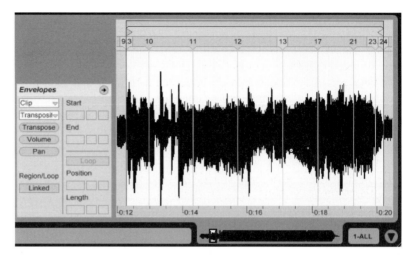

mal speed until it hit bar 5, then it would grind to an almost-halt. Then I got busy with the clip transposition envelope; see the screen shot for how it looked. This removed the last traces of humanity from the stretched clip, adding a creepy synthesised quality – which is a good thing.

Stretched audio sample with transposition automation

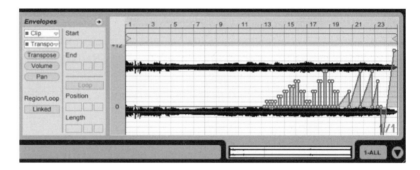

Close up of transposition

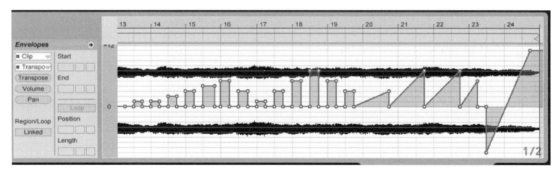

- Clip envelopes are 'burned in' to your new audio file when you consolidate a clip.
- Clip envelopes aren't reversed when you reverse an audio clip. If you reverse a clip that fades out, it'll still fade out!

Automating the cross fader

Live's cross fader movements can of course be recorded during a performance, and edited (if necessary) later. The cross fader is interesting for non-DJs too – you can use it to create new beats and sounds, and the automation helps with this. Drop 3 different beats into a Live set – one beat per

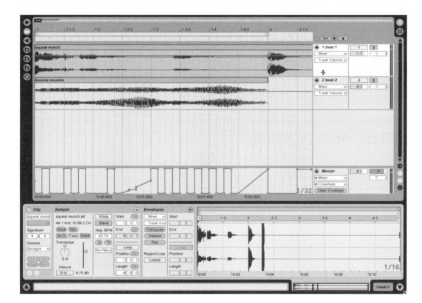

Crossfader automation

track. Add some other sound like speech on track 4. Assign some of the sounds to Deck A, and the rest to Deck B, play with the crossfader to see what happens, using either your mouse or a hardware fader/knob. Then record your cross fader moves in real time, or draw them in; this only needs to be over a couple of bars. Play it back – find a part that sounds good, then bounce it to another track, and use it as a fresh beat/loop.

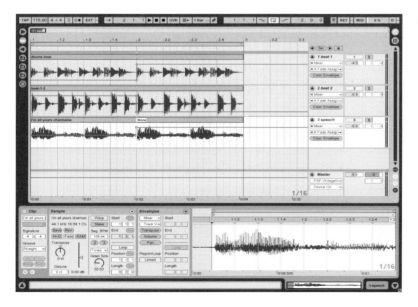

Crossfader 'deck' assignment

- You don't have to be using beats for this – mix together any interesting sounds.
- You can also automate the A-B assignment, so a clip can jump decks as it goes on.

Song tempo automation

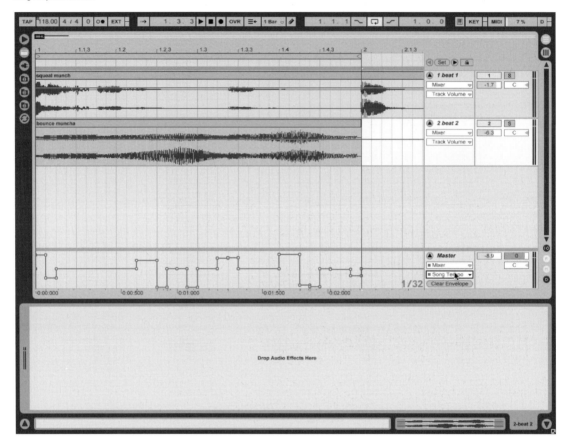

- Go further: do a micro version, over one bar, using short noise loops, and draw in a lot of fast crossfader assignments. Set the loops to Repitch, then draw in some tempo changes over that bar. This can get quite messed up – which is, yes, good.

Envelopes in tracks – the Arrangement View

Generally, using automation in tracks is the same as working in clips – drawing, editing, copying, etc. There's a useful 'Clear Envelope' button in the Arrangement View mixer, and a 'Delete Envelope' command in the Edit menu.

The back to arrangement button

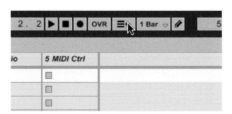

Info – the BTA button

You need to understand the Back To Arrangement button, in Live's Control Bar. Visible from either view, it turns red when you depart from your recorded Arrangement – a track can't play an Arrangement and a Session part simultaneously, and Session is prioritised. If you're playing back a song and something isn't working like it should, click on this little fella and your problems will go away! This is useful if you're jamming in Arrangement View, and flip to Session View to trigger a particular clip. The BTA button will 'light', and regular automation/playback for that track will cease, as the newly-triggered clip takes over. When you want to return to the regular Arrangement, click the BTA button, and Live will pickup exactly where it should be according to the Arrangement View timeline.

Versatile envelopes

Automation envelopes are really versatile, there's so many ways you can work with them:

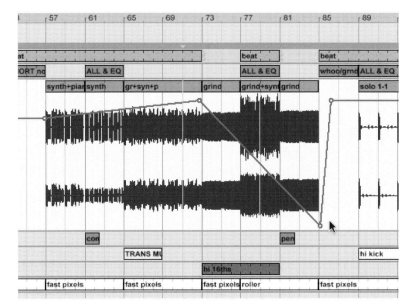

Selection automation to copy

- Copy an envelope you've drawn for one parameter, and paste it onto another, just to see what happens. You can also do this across different instruments and mixer functions.
- Click and drag around part of an envelope to move it to a new location. The remaining portion will stretch at the connection point.
- Use copy and paste to duplicate sections of an envelope, to save drawing in long/repetitive sections.
- You can copy an envelope from a track to a clip, and vice versa.
- Unlink an envelope from a looping clip so they can both run over different lengths, like 8 bars of clip automation on a 1 bar clip – if it's a suitable parameter, you'll hear a cumulative effect as the looping goes on.

Envelopes in the Library

If you really enjoy drawing in complicated curves, you could create a folder in your Library for Live Clips with automation envelopes that you could reload and reuse; it's not unusual for Logic users to create 'favourite' envelopes that they use repeatedly.

About the views

Left brain, right brain...

The relationship between the Session and Arrangement Views is a fundamental part of the Live experience, and you have to get to grips with it. Occasionally I run into people who work in only one View, and they're surprised when I mention what's possible in the other; it's very common that people who come to Live from Cubase or Pro Tools or whatever, gravitate to the Arrangement View, and just sit there – which is fine, but they won't be getting the most out of Live. Moving between Session and Arrangement requires nothing more than a tap of the tab key, and working in one doesn't mean you're forbidden from popping round the corner to visit the other.

Live Session View

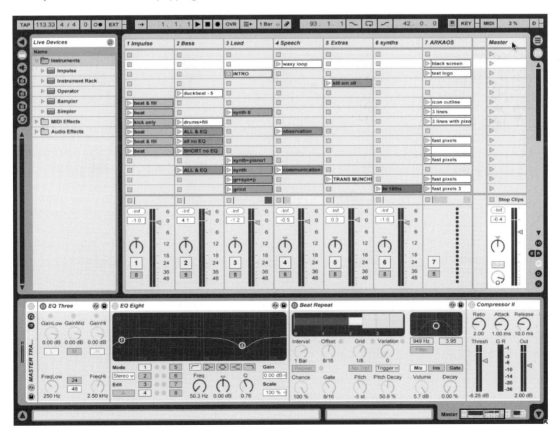

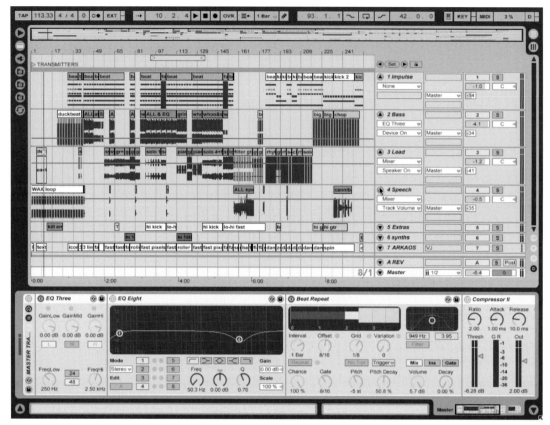

Arrangement View

Defining the Views can be a problem – not technically, but conceptually. Think of the two sides of the human brain – the left side is said to be the creative, spontaneous side, and the right is the practical, logical side. They work together in harmony to create a well-rounded, fully-functioning brain (er...on a good day). The Session View is Live's left brain – you can compile your audio material from various sources, drag'n'drop clips at will, experiment with crazy signal routings, make pretty musical patterns, arrange your clips into scenes, and jam around with intuitive song structures. Anything goes – this is Live as an instrument. The Arrangement View is Live's right brain. It's where you record and organise those improvised structures, add more automation, rearrange parts, lay out your song's final arrangement, and mix in preparation for rendering the finished song. View your composition in a linear fashion, along a more 'traditional'-looking timeline ranging from left to right. Of course, you can still drag'n'drop new material, and perform tweaks and edits while Live is running, but it feels quite different from the Session View.

Hardcore Session users might be surprised to hear that some people jam in the Arrangement View, which is just weird...or is it? We'll get to that soon...

Live talks to itself

We all know how simple Live is to use. It's like a game – challenging you to make connections, to exceed the simplicity and do really strange things. One of these things is something I came across by mistake – and now I use it, I can't imagine it not being there, so it qualifies as useful and strange.

Live can send MIDI to itself

You can send notes or CC's from a MIDI track in Live, to all of the other tracks in Live – I'm sorry to say that once again Mac users have the advantage here; this is all about sending MIDI out from – and then back into – Live itself, something that's very easy to do with the IAC Bus in Mac OSX, but which requires third-party help

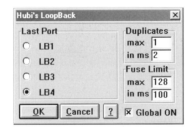

Hubi MIDI LoopBack

under Windows; you could try something like Hubi's MIDI LoopBack or MIDI Ox. So far there are two major uses that I have for this, one very practical and the other quite crazy, and I'll detail them here. I'm not trying to tease you or give it a big build up, I just want to make sure I explain it clearly. And be careful – avoid

MIDI Ox website

IAC Driver in Audio MIDI Setup

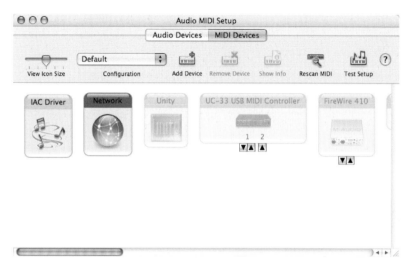

getting into MIDI feedback where you have MIDI being sent and received by the same application – you can get into serious hang-ups!

Info – what is the IAC Bus?

The Mac OSX IAC Bus is something that you might never have encountered. 'IAC' stands for Inter Application Communication; if you remember OMS under Mac OS9, then – basically – this is it. Open Audio MIDI Setup in the Utilities folder, and click on the 'MIDI Devices' tab. You'll see icons representing various MIDI devices; ignore them and click on the icon for IAC Driver. In the resulting pop-up, make sure 'Device is online' is ticked, and there's at least one port in the list (you can create more than one port if you need it). That's all you have to do with the IAC – just make sure it's on! If you've made any changes, click 'Apply', then quit Audio MIDI Setup.

IAC properties

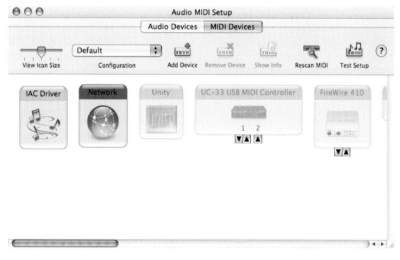

Song setup clips

This is the most 'useful' of my two MIDI stunts. The aim here is to create a MIDI clip to go at the top of each new song in a Live set. When triggered the clip will send 'jump to' messages to Live's mixer settings, in preparation for

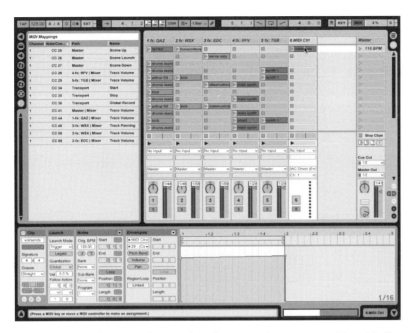

Setup clip at top right 'vol/sends', with relevant MIDI controllers selected throughout Session View.

the next song – for example restoring all pans to the centre position; it's like loading a preset on a digital mixer. If you're working through a Live set that contains several songs, it means that one click sets you up for the next song – avoiding a lot of mousework.

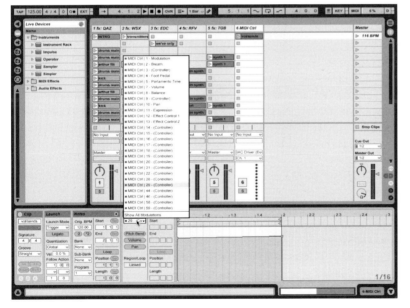

MIDI controllers being selected and edited in Live

As long as your IAC Bus is active, it'll appear as an output destination beneath a MIDI track. Then go to Preferences and make sure the IAC Bus is listed as an Active Device in the MIDI/Sync tab. Select 'Track' and 'Remote' in both the Active Device Input and Output slots. Now any MIDI messages sent from your MIDI track will go in a loop courtesy of the IAC Bus.

Showing IAC Bus as Live MIDI destination

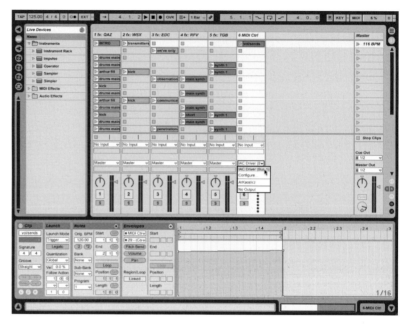

Slight drawback: you need a MIDI hardware controller to map the MIDI controllers in Live in the first place. Once you've done that, you can then enter the necessary MIDI controller numbers and parameter changes in your Live clip – see the screen shot for this, and see 'Automation'. It means that you can leave the hardware at home when you go out to play.

- Even when sending a '0' message, it's necessary to put in an incremental change, however small; otherwise Live doesn't pick it up.

It's important to avoid sending too much MIDI information at the same time – as long as you're sending simple mixer resets, that should be okay. If you do run into any problems, try staggering the MIDI info, sending different elements at slightly different times, or split it up to send on different channels.

Once you've got your 'reset' clip or clips sorted out, don't forget to drag them into the Library, so you can use them in future Live sets – the MIDI information will be stored as part of the Live Clip format. Remember to name them something useful!

Even if you're using a hardware controller like the FCB1010 pedal board, or an Ozonic, this is still worthwhile, because it puts this 'reset' on one button or key.

The MIDI mangler

The aim here is to take this Live-MIDI-to-Live thing as far as it can go, but still to produce a usable result. My experience with the 'reset' MIDI clip led me to ask some new questions:

- Is it possible to combine this technique with follow actions to automate Live's clips to an extreme degree?

- Can Live be persuaded to play audio clips randomly, while also randomly changing mixer and effect parameters – and record the result without human intervention?

Of course the answer to these questions is 'yes', otherwise the paragraph above that would have been the end of this chapter. What I wanted to do was create a 'processor', based on follow actions and effects; something that would enable any two audio clips to be dropped in and mashed up, but which would produce different results every time; it's a work in progress, but this is where I'm up to.

First, all previous comments about Audio MIDI Setup and the IAC Bus apply. Then, refer to the screen shot of the finished article, it'll make the explanations a lot clearer. This Live set is based on the limitations of putting it together on my PowerBook; you might find that you can get it working on more, or fewer, simultaneous tracks, depending on your set-up.

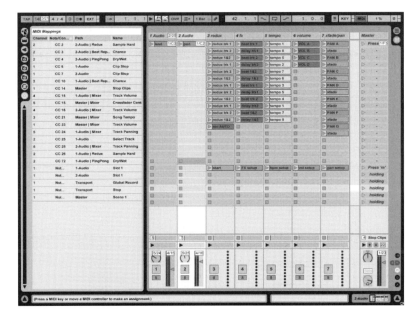

Session View with MIDI mapping visible

- In Session View, I use two audio tracks, and five MIDI tracks.
- Each audio track has Redux, Beat Repeat, and Ping Pong Delay effects loaded.
- I mapped MIDI controllers to one function of each effect.
- I mapped MIDI controllers to the project tempo, the faders and pan pots of the audio tracks, and MIDI notes to the 'stop' and 'record' buttons.
- Each MIDI track contains a number of MIDI clips, each group of clips sending controllers to specific parameters. These include: Redux Downsample rate, Beat Repeat Chance, Ping Pong Dry/Wet Mix, tempo, crossfade, and Track 1/2 volume and pan. Different clips in each MIDI track send different parameters, so the same parameters aren't being triggered over and over.
- I've applied follow actions to the clips in each MIDI track. I used the

Session View with computer keyboard mapping visible

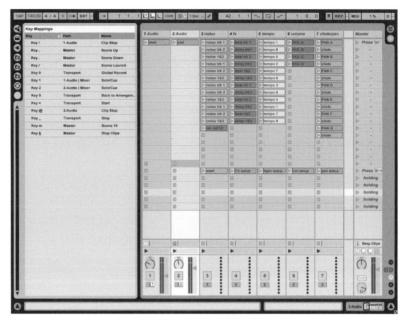

same settings for most of them: 'Any' and '50'; but in track 7 I used 'Next' to alternate between pan and crossfade.
- A few empty scenes below the follow action clips, I have a starting scene. This is similar to the MIDI 'song header' clips I mentioned earlier. The clips in this scene restore 'default' settings to the Live set. The leftmost clip 'start', sends a MIDI note to trigger the top scene in the Live set.
- I dropped one clip into the top slot of each audio track. It's important to prepare these clips properly – they must be set to 'loop', and the 'Re-pitch' warp mode should be selected.

The finished result in progress, with follow actions

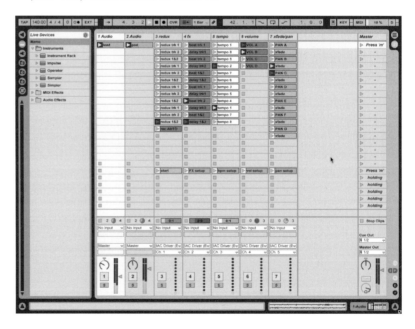

- I mapped the letter 'm' to trigger my starting scene. When I press 'm', the MIDI note is sent to trigger the top scene, triggering the audio clips in the audio tracks, and the top follow action MIDI clips.
- That starts the thing off. As the follow actions trigger the MIDI clips, various MIDI controllers are sent. Effects parameters change, the mixer fades and pans automatically, and the entire 'song' speeds up and slows down.
- I saved the best until last; the final follow action clip in track one sends two MIDI notes – the first starts recording, and – one bar later – the second stops the entire track.
- This means that at a random point, this automated Live set starts and stops recording on it's own; taking the whole process out of your hands.
- That's cool!
- Hit tab to go into Arrangement View, and look at what Live has recorded for you. At this point, disable all of the IAC outputs, so when you play back the recording, Live isn't still sending MIDI. Render it to disk as a separate file.
- I like this stuff – you can put in long or short clips, speech, beats, noises, instrument sounds; that's up to you. The Re-pitch setting is really important, because it works in tandem with the song BPM to drastically change the sound of the clips; instead of retaining their pitch as the song BPM changes, they 'speed up' and 'slow down', like vinyl.
- The record clip is the killer for me, but if you just want to keep it playing forever, just move that clip out of the follow action group. You could make longer recordings by creating longer record clips.
- Keep the new loops that you create by doing this; drop them into your future Live sets, and chop 'em up and warp them all over again!
- You might notice on the screen shot that each MIDI track sends on a different channel; an attempt to avoid clogging up channel 1.

Two clips go in one end, and come out the other end very mashed up! I hope this makes sense – it should at least give you ideas about things to try yourself.

Maybe you could use this in a performance situation, combining it with manually-triggered clips, and with the help of a hardware controller like the UC33e; though you'd have to make sure that your controller isn't sending on a channel that's already in use.

I have to say – try this at your own risk. I did find that Live got badly frozen up when I was trying to send too much info at once (no permanent damage done); that's why I settled on the layout seen here.

After this? It opens a lot of doors. The use of follow actions to 'time' a recording is quite interesting, don't you think? You can have huge cascades of MIDI clips and follow actions.

This demonstrates what I've been saying about Live – it's like a game, building new connections from simple functions – whatever next?!

Performance notes

Live is like one of those Transformers from the cartoons; in the studio it's a full-blown DAW, used for writing and production, then on stage it transforms into an instrument, with a very workable interface and real-time control over all functions. In a performance context, Live resembles the grooveboxes of old, but applies the philosophy to both MIDI and audio content in a way that hardware devices could only dream of (if they could only dream). Yamaha came close, with their RM1x and RS7000, and their Motif keyboard range features some attributes of both of these, but they're different beasts from Live; they can't provide the same level of creative freedom.

The arguments about the validity of performing with computers are over. Computers crash, guitar strings break, singers fall off the stage and break their necks...I'd rather reboot my computer in front of an audience than re-string my bass – I know which would be faster too. And, guitar-playing technophobes – a Les Paul is the product of vast amounts of industrial power; if you want true low-tech, go bang some rocks together.

If you're standing in front of an audience, and you're doing something where you have the potential to make great mistakes as well as great music – that counts as a performance.

A set for every song, or every song in the set?

Live users love to find the 'ultimate' way to do things – of course, there is no ultimate; in our field, things are changing constantly. Today's 'ultimate' audio interface is doomed to spend a lot of tomorrows getting dusty on the shelf, and a lot of day-after-tomorrows in the garage, with our Yamaha QY10s.

One of our fruitless quests involves the construction of 'ultimate' Live sets for performance use – I guess you might call them Live live sets. There are so many ways to do this, and that's a good thing. The first thing to appreciate is that, although only one Live document can be open at a time, there's no need to have a separate Live set for every song. It's possible to have several songs structured vertically in one Session View, and use Live's BPM scene changes, channel changes from a keyboard/controller, and something like my Live song header idea – explained in' Live Talks To Itself!' – to work through the evening's set (DJs who like to work with an entire song per clip can disregard all of this).

We also have the ability to drag entire Live sets (or selected parts) from the File Browser into the current set. This is a fantastic development – it makes it much easier to mix and match songs, or parts of songs, and the

> **Info**
>
> Don't keep changing your set-up – if you get something that works, stick with it for a while, give yourself time to learn it inside-out.

Live sets being dropped into each other

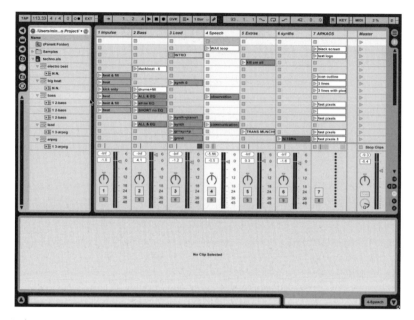

adventurous spirit can go on stage with nothing on screen (or maybe an opening song), then drop in everything else from the Browser as the set progresses; you won't encounter any audio dropouts when you do this, but if you drop in a big set, there can be quite a wait for it to load, during which time you can't do anything in Live.

If you want to drag'n'drop sets into each other, you'll need a consistent structure for them – controller mapping, number of tracks, and effects used should remain constant, but many users stick to a common pattern in their performance sets anyway, saving the 'irregular' stuff for studio/home work/experimentation.

I work with a hybrid approach – I go on stage with most of my required songs loaded, but I also have a selection of 'spares' bookmarked in the File Browser, so I can go off on a tangent if I want to.

Prepare your set for performance

However you decide to build your set, there are things you can do to make it more performance-friendly.

- Pre render all software instrument clips – take the load off!
- Remember that you can change the width of tracks in the Session View – spread them out to fill the available space and to make your clip labelling more visible.
- Consider lowering your screen resolution for on-stage use. What you lose in 'real estate', you gain in clarity. I used to do this, though I had to abandon it when I started ReWiring to Arkaos VJ – just couldn't fit it all in!
- Label everything. Clips for sure, but the tracks too – I label mine with the letters that I need to trigger effects on that particular track. So if I have EQ and Beat Repeat on track 1, and Q and W will toggle those effects on/off, I name the track Q/W.

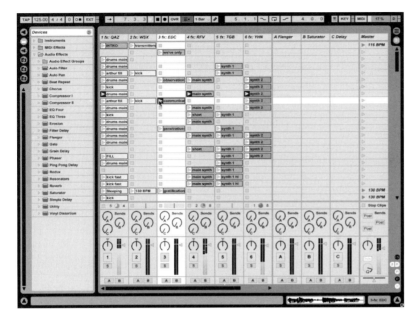

An example of the author's Live sets

- Colour coding is helpful too – anything that gives you more information on screen at a quick glance. I have my own system - whenever I see a white clip, for example, I know it's a drum loop; blue is speech or vocals, green is bass, and so on.
- I set my global quantization to 1 bar for stage use. It gives me plenty of time to trigger the next clip or scene; a bar is a long time!
- My songs are quite structured, but I always throw a few extra loops and one-shots into the set, usually as transitions in-between songs. It's a good chance to try out new loops and sounds on stage before incorporating them into 'proper' songs.
- When you rehearse your set, set everything up as you will on stage – with all interfaces connected, and any ReWired applications that you intend to use. These will put a drain on your computer, and you should find out how much of a drain before – not during – the performance.
- If you've been tweaking your latency/buffer settings in Live's preferences, you may need to change these settings for performance use.

Song header scenes
Read about song header scenes in Chapter 4 – very useful when working with big sets on stage.

Onstage troubleshooting
Some quick 'look outs' for stage use:

- Using a hardware controller on stage adds another layer of things to do. Take the M-Audio Ozonic as an example; you need to set this one up extra carefully – your audio's coming out of it too! The Ozonic is FireWire-based, and must be connected while the computer is off. Once the computer restarts, launch Live, and make sure the Ozonic is

identified correctly; if necessary go to Audio and MIDI preferences, and select the Ozonic as the output/input source. Make sure you have the correct preset loaded on the Ozonic. Make sure the Ozonic's volume controllers are at the appropriate starting positions, and you've connected all necessary inputs/outputs at the back of the keyboard. Whatever device you use, you'll have to get into some sort of routine like this – that's one reason why I don't like to change my setup too often.
- Remember to connect your audio interface (a friend-who-shall-be-nameless forgot to do this at Cargo in London recently – long silence at the beginning of his set).
- Do you want to tweak your audio interface's knobs during the set? Don't put it on the floor, then.
- Getting interference? Try running your laptop from the battery instead of mains power.
- Remember to select your interface as input/output in Live's preferences.
- Go easy on hungry plug-ins. Maybe you should pre-render instruments and effects before the gig.
- Don't freeze or unfreeze tracks during your set – freezing will stop all audio, and unfreezing can produce pops or clicks.

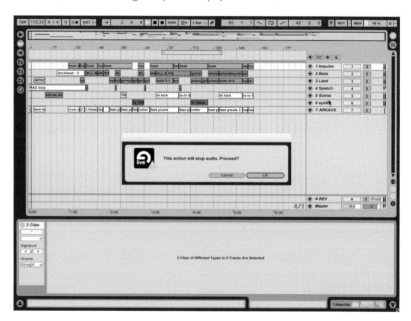

Live track freezing in progress

- Oops! The Sudden Silence Syndrome: have you soloed a track? Have you got a filter or gate at an extreme setting?
- Most important, remember to have fun. You're quite safe with Live – it's very stable. What's the worst that could happen? Enjoy it…

Device racks in a live situation

Although they're a powerful tool for creating synth sounds in the studio, device racks are also invaluable in live situations. Let's take drums, for example; you can proceed through different Impulse setups in your set, without

New device rack, with Impulse loaded

having to ever manually load a new preset; all you need are some MIDI CCs...

Create a new MIDI track, and drop in Impulse. Control-click on the Impulse title bar, and choose 'create group'. A small bar will appear at the left of Impulse, with the generic title 'Instrument Rack'. There are 4 buttons on this bar, make sure they are all active (highlighted); as you do this, the rack will expand to reveal all of its components.

At the left, there are the eight Macro knobs which can be freely assigned to multiple parameters, we'll get back to those later. Next to those, the Chain List, and then of course the Impulse device. We need to load some Impulse presets now, if you haven't got any of your own, just use some from the Library, doesn't really matter which ones.

Use the preset hot-swap button to load an Impulse preset. Then go to the Browser, find another Impulse preset, and drag it straight into the empty space in the Chain List. Yep, right where it says 'Drop MIDI Effects, Audio Effects or Instruments Here'. Repeat this with 3 other presets, and you'll end up with a Chain List that includes 5 chains. Each chain represents a different instance of Impulse. If you click on a chain, you'll see the Impulse device changing to reflect the newly-selected preset (some of the differences may be quite subtle, so keep a sharp eye out).

You can use the context menu to rename these chains. Let's assume you want one Impulse kit for each song in your set. Name the first chain 'Song 1', the second 'Song 2', and so on. Now you have a set list for your virtual drummer.

Above the Chain List is a button called 'Chain', click on this. Now you can define a Chain Select Zone for each of your kits/songs. You do this by dragging zones to the right in the Zone Editor. The short way to explain this is to say: refer to the screen shot overleaf, to see the finished result. The numbers across the top are MIDI controller values, from 0 to 127. Note that none of the zones I've created overlap, very important, otherwise you'll get two kits triggering at once, unless that's what you want. These zones are defining which MIDI controller values will trigger which Impulse kit. This would work the same way if we were using Operator, Simpler, whatever.

Our next assumption is that you've already programmed some MIDI clips containing drum parts for your songs, and that they're in the Impulse track. As you move through your set, you may be triggering these clips specifically, or they may be triggered as part of a scene – either one is good.

Select the first MIDI drum clip you want to use in your set, we need to be able to see it in the Clip View. If necessary, click the small E near the lower

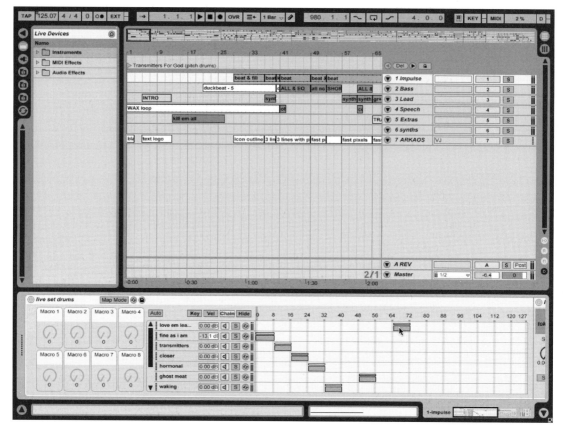

Device rack chain zone editor

left of the Clip View, to display the Envelope View, because that's what we need to work on. Click in the Device Chooser box, and choose your rack from the pop-up list. If you've renamed it, it'll display that name, otherwise it'll just say 'Instrument Rack'. The small box below the Device Chooser is the Control Chooser – from here choose Chain Selector. Draw in an envelope within the value range defined by your first zone...again, see the screen shot for clarification. This means that whenever the clip is launched, it will send that controller value, ensuring that whenever you play that clip from song 1, the appropriate sounds will be loaded.

Repeat this procedure with the first clips in every song, applying the correct controller values. If you like to jam around during your set, and you may launch these clips in a different order, simply insert these controller values into every drum clip in your set, so you can never go wrong – you'll always get the correct sounds for the part.

You also have the option of applying a crossfader to these zones using the even smaller bar at the top of each zone...then you might assign a MIDI control to create crossfades between different sounds; probably not so often with drums, but it can sound great with synths.

Each of these chains could also contain it's own assortment of audio and MIDI effects. It's a great way to have ever-changing automated sounds within in a single Live track.

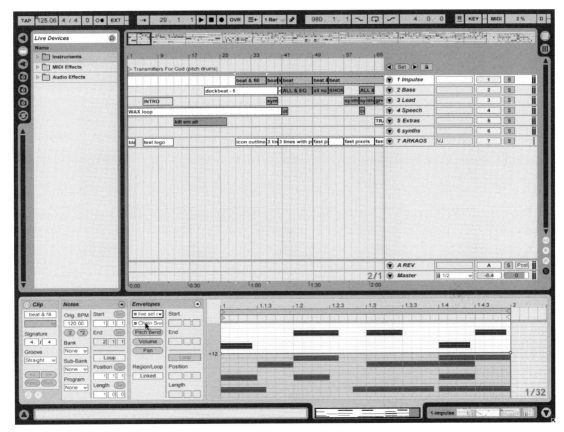

Controller value being entered in MIDI

As for those Macro knobs, they give us a handy way to map one knob to several different device parameters, so you don't have to delve within the rack every time you want to transpose a drum sound, or an entire kit, or tweak an effects level...it gives you a layer of control right at the top of the pile. Very useful!

Solo performance – J-Lab

J-Lab is one of the UK's most experienced Live performers; performing regularly at assorted clubs and dives around London. I've seen him jamming with other laptop musicians, and performing lengthy solo sets. Here he shares some thoughts on solo performance with Live:

> **Quote**
>
> 'I come from a background of using Cubase on the Atari, and then on Macs I've worked with Reason and Reaktor. I use Live 100% in live situations, about 75% in the studio. Most of my writing comes from a performance/improvisation angle, and since Live gained MIDI and VST/AU support, it's made Logic redundant for writing – though I still use it for mixing and mastering. Alongside Live I use Reason, radiaL, Pluggo, FM7, Pro53, Absynth, and PSP's Vintage Warmer. For hardware control I use a Novation Remote 25 and Motu 828 FireWire audio interface. Most of the sounds I use are recorded and composed by me. Any third-party samples get manipulated in some way – years of programming an E-MU 64 and fear of litigation turned me into a compulsive sample mangler! – *J-Lab*

J-Lab performing

Generally I run 8 tracks live – my old G3 couldn't cope with more, and it's still a nice number for the new machine! For my techno stuff, the tracks are laid out like this:

1. Hard beats
2. Softer beats (with a filter and Beat Repeat)
3. Percussive/abstract rhythm (with a gate)
4. Bass (with a filter)
5. Lead (with a filter)
6. Secondary lead/harmony
7. Secondary lead/harmony
8. Weirdness and soundbites

I use three auxs – a mega 'performance' delay, a normal delay sharing with the Ableton Reverb, and whatever I feel like on the third aux. The hard rhythm and bass run compressors. All the other plug-ins are switchable, a legacy of using an old laptop for ages, but this system has allowed me to accommodate most of the functionality on the controller keyboard and get away from the laptop in the gig. All my clips are from tracks I've written or bits I'm messing with. There's no pre-arrangement, I just fire off whatever, and take it from there. No two gigs are ever the same, and normally something completely new comes out of them. To make it more interesting I quantize to an eighth note, so I can create new rhythmic possibilities. Live is so intuitive, it leaves the computer and sits in my head, leaving me to get on with the music.' *J-Lab*

Info – select a track with a MIDI note

You can use MIDI notes to select Live's tracks – used in conjunction with the scene scroll and select functions (also assignable) this gives you a way to navigate around tracks, scenes, and clips without touching the computer keyboard.

Chapter 10: Performance notes   83

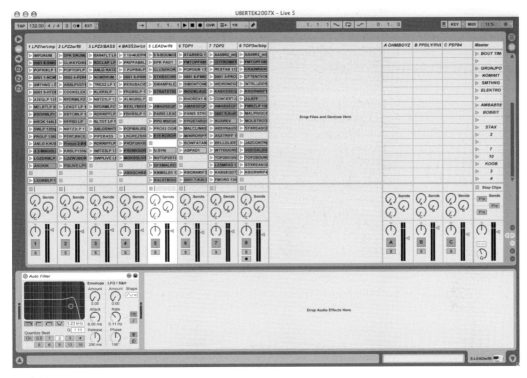

J-Lab's Live sets

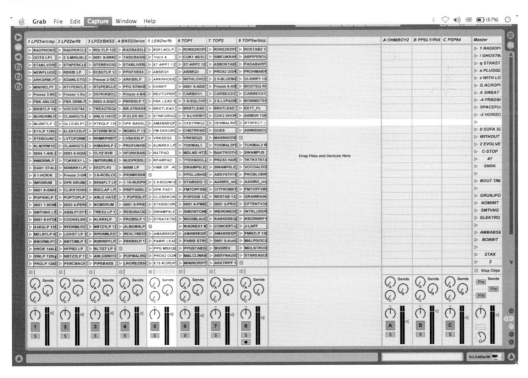

Using Live within a band – Songcarver/Keith Lang

Australian Keith Lang is another experienced Live performer, using it in his own solo sets as Songcarver, as well as in a band capacity. Keith is co-creator of Musolomo, a real-time VST performance sampler, which works within Live:

> **Quote**
>
> 'I use Live to trigger loops and play keyboard parts, and to process live guitar as part of a 5-piece pop/dance/funk band called Cocoa Jackson Lane. Generally the plug-ins I use are Musolomo – of course – and the MDA combo guitar distortion; sometimes a few others, all freebies. In the studio I also use the Logic instruments which were part of Logic 6. I use a Novation Remote25 MIDI controller, and a Motu 828 FireWire audio interface, alongside a few custom items.
>
> I never use pre-made loops – all my sounds are from instruments or highly-edited 'natural' recordings – like me banging on pots and pans in the kitchen. I put all the songs in a single set, and my Novation has a bunch of 'sets' in it, which means the MIDI output changes for each 'set' I choose on my MIDI controller; Live just sits there and listens.
>
> I usually group the loop-based stuff into five 'sections'. It's all triggered with no quantization and I have a cool custom setup for tempo which allows me to use some buttons for push/ pull and increase and decrease tempo by 2.5 bpm. There are times in the band context when I'm conscious of some of Live's shortcomings: time signature changes suck, and tempo changes are pretty blocky. It's very much a 4/4, block of 8 bars sort of thinking – the culture of dance music. It doesn't encourage a sense of harmonic progression.' – *Keith Lang*

Freeze tracks in the Session View

You can freeze tracks in the Session View, as well as the Arrangement View – the frozen track will be highlighted; see the screen shot. Clips will still launch and the mixer controls will still function, but you can't go into the clip to change anything. Perhaps you could use track freeze like this if you've got a software instrument track in your Live set and you don't want to bother bouncing all the clips down to audio files.

Jamming in the Arrangement View is just wrong

Because Live is so real-time oriented, it's possible to do a lot of jamming-type actions in the Arrangement View. The first time I saw Ergo Phizmiz do this, I must admit I was surprised, but there's always some crossover between Live's Views, and I guess this is a reflection of that. Certainly you can drag and drop your way around the Arrangement View, but in general the Session View is the place to improvise; although Live's locators only serve to encourage this kind of behaviour – allowing quantized movement between song sections, and real-time restructuring in the Arrangement View... hey, that sounds interesting... now they've got me at it...

- You can't record locator jumps as part of the automation in the Arrangement View.

Locators in the Arrangement View

Live in the theatre

Live has also found a place in theatres, where its real-time operation means that music and sound effects can be delivered on cue, even if the cue doesn't quite come where it should! I had a quick word with Joe Young, who knows more about this sort of thing than I do:

Quote

'I use Live only in performance – I use ProTools and radiaL for studio work. My hardware setup is a Pro Tools MBox and M-Audio Ozone controller keyboard. I use my own environmental sound recordings, plus samples from various sources – CD, vinyl, etc. I limit myself to 8 tracks of audio, so that I have enough hardware control on the Ozone. I have a rough score already worked out from rehearsals, and then I intuitively feed the sounds in during performance; I appreciate the ability to have a large number of pre-loaded sounds mapped and ready for performance. I see Live as a very sophisticated playback and processing machine, rather than an instrument.' *Joe Young*

VJing – video performance alongside Live

See Chapter 15 for information about using Live with the popular Arkaos VJ software. You might want to also look at Chapter 13 to read about Live's new found ability to import and display video.

Info – shopping

If you're going on stage with Live, get a gooseneck-style USB light – it's probably the most useful piece of hardware you'll ever buy. I also like the MicFlex from MacMice – not a 'serious' studio tool, but good for anybody who wants to talk or do some vocal processing on stage. Plug in the MicFlex, and it appears in Live's preferences as an Input Audio Device called C-Media USB Headphone set (1 In, 0 Out). Go to an audio track in Live and choose Ext. In, then '1' rather than the more usual '1/2', and arm the track to record.

Info – recording and rendering your set

Because it's so easy to do in Live, many Live performers record their sets. Just click the record button and everything you do will be recorded – clip launches, mixer moves, effect moves. I nearly always forget to do this. But it is useful, to be able to listen to your sets afterwards...for evaluation, and for burning CDs for promotion or your entertainment...or your friends' entertainment. By viewing your set in the arrangement view you can see and hear how you're structuring your sets over the time. The rendering procedure: select all, or click and drag around the section you want to render. Then shift-command-r to see the render window. The options are basic – explain format, normalisation, stereo/mono, etc. Then click OK, name your file, and rendering begins. How long rendering takes depends on: how long the set is, and how many effects were used. Selecting the normalisation option adds another step to the process, as Live has to go through the entire set first looking for the loudest section, before rendering can begin.

DJing notes

Why is Live good for DJs?
I don't think it was planned that way, but Live is great for DJing. The DJs started to come on board early – some of the world's leading DJs are Live's most vocal supporters – and their input has influenced Live's development; we all benefit from the new features that this has inspired. In fact, that's the reason why this section on DJing is so brief – everything in this book is relevant to DJing, just as it is to performance, or composition, or whatever else you're doing. See for example the section on mashups in 'Studio Notes'; or the section on the File Browser in 'Get Organised'…

Live's had DJ-friendly features for, well, forever, it seems: the way that entire songs can be browsed and dropped in as single clips, or cut into sections, and beat-matched by use of the warp markers; the pre-listening options; tap tempo; and of course the crossfader. Or how about features like Auto-Warping, where entire songs (or long samples) are automatically issued with warp markers when they're imported; Complex warp mode, for material containing a mixture of beats and melodic parts; Re-Pitch warp mode for more vinyl-like behaviour of audio clips; and nudge, where a looping clip's start point can be bumped backwards or forwards.

When DJs started using Live, they often tried to create a Live set which somehow related to their twin record decks, based around a two-track system, with DJ-friendly plug-ins like EQ3 and Auto Filter; this has changed, however, as DJs have come to appreciate Live's power – the truth is, anything goes. I already mentioned the sections on mashups and the File Browser; you should also read about labelling clips and tracks in Chapter 4, mapping and hardware controllers in Chapter 16, the Complex warp mode in Chapter 4, and Chapter 9, building Live sets in Chapter 10, and the crossfader in Chapter 7.

That Re-Pitch mode – it's funny, after going to all that trouble to stretch audio in a natural way, now we want it to change pitch with tempo again. Whether you're a DJ or not, Re-Pitch is a useful creative effect, and sound mangling just wouldn't be the same without it (see Chapter 9).

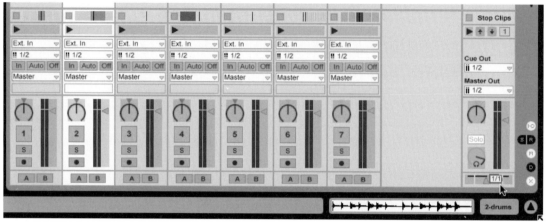

Live's cross fader

Live DJing with Jody Wisternoff (Way Out West)

'I love the way you can click on a section of audio and adjust the pitch straight away; really useful for fine tuning samples; DigiDesign take note! Planning DJ sets and making DJ mixes has never been easier and quicker. The Auto Warp function is 99% accurate, and the task of beat matching audio is radically simplified – serious time saver!

I use the M-Audio Oxygen 8 keyboard, because it is portable and straightforward; I also use the Evolution UC-33 for the same reasons. The M-Audio FW410 is my audio interface; it is very reliable.'

Pre listening/Cueing

If you're using an audio interface like the Echo AudioFire2, with at least 2 stereo pairs, you can configure it with Live for cueing (or pre-listening, as it's also known), like a DJ mixer. Audio in the Browser, and in selected tracks, can be monitored on, say, tracks 3+4, while the main mix goes to the PA on tracks 1+2. Use the Cue Out button to set this up – click on it, then choose Configure... which will open the Audio panel in Preferences. Then choose Channel Configuration/Output Config. Now you'll see a list of your hardware's outputs – make sure 1/2 (stereo) and 3/4 (stereo) are highlighted, then click OK, and close the windows. The knob below master track pan is your cue volume control, the button above that switches between solo mode and cue mode – when solo mode is engaged, the solo switches work as usual across the mixer, silencing all tracks other than those that are soloed. When cue mode is engaged, however, all output from the browser, and any soloed tracks can be pre listened on outputs 3 and 4.

> **Tip**
>
> Mac OSX users can set-up for cueing even if their interface doesn't have the necessary facilities. See Chapter 17.

MIDI hardware setup

More than with any other type of Ableton-based performance, hardware control is essential for DJs... if you want to emulate, or improve on, the hands-on experience of working with vinyl decks and DJ mixers, a well-chosen hardware controller will make all the difference. There are a lot of hardware controllers out there, that are suitable for DJ use; in most ways, it's not much different than for any other use. Sometimes though, DJs want something small, that will fit into a cramped DJ booth; they also tend to be more conscious of build quality than the average studio/home-bound user. And then of course there's the crossfader. From what I've seen with Live students, most who are new to the idea of DJing with Live are quite insistent that they have a crossfader. However, once they venture beyond the old-fashioned two-track setup, most lose interest in using a crossfader, and become more concerned with buttons, knobs, and mixer-style faders. While we're on the crossfader subject though, see the 'automation' chapter for some fun with automating the crossfader

Info – resize your tracks

If you're working on a DJ set that's only using 2 or 3 or 6 tracks...you can resize Live tracks to make the most of available screen space, by dragging them wider in the Session View track title bar. it will allow you to give clips and tracks longer, more descriptive names, if nothing else.

Live DJing with Tarekith

Chicago-based Tarekith is one of the most knowledgeable Live users around, equally at home in the fields of DJing and production.

Live DJing with Tarekith

'I consider myself primariy a producer, but I've been DJing and doing Live PA's for almost as long as I've been writing music. Been doing electronic music for about 14 years now, though I was heavily into the guitar for 3 or 4 years before that.

Before Live came along, like most DJs, I was using 1200's and a regular DJ mixer. I was always incorporating my production gear into my DJing though, things like the Roland MC505 and SP808, Korg ER-1, and Emu Command Stations. Even an Akai S3000XL for awhile there.

Live opens up a lot of possibilities for me in terms of what kind of music I can play. I'm not stuck using only tunes that had been released on vinyl, if it's audio in any form, I can now use it in my DJ sets in a very fluid way.

It's easier to find tracks I want to play, I can set up my 'virtual dj booth' the way I want in terms of how many channels I want to use, or effects I like. Personally I think DJing with a laptop sounds much better than vinyl, though you do need to stay within certain tempo limits to achieve that, (not using songs too far from their original tempo).

I still like doing the actual mixing of my DJ sets with my Allen & Heath Xone62, I just prefer the feel and sound of its EQ and fader to a MIDI controller. My main controller for effects and triggering is the Kenton Killamix Mini, and every so often I'll add my Elektron Machinedrum-UW into the mix as well.

I really enjoy setting up my own custom Live Racks, making my own effects that not only sound the way I want, but function the way I want as well. That and the ability to see precisely where certain sections of a song are while playing is a huge advantage, I can really time every aspect of a set as much as I want. This opens up a lot of creative possibilities for me while mixing, and lets me create more cohesive DJ sets.

I've used the Sampler and Simpler devices for dropping in the odd sample, but to be honest I'm one of those DJs who prefers to let the songs speak for themselves most of the time. A good song is all you need to make a good party, so I prefer to play things as the producer intended, and not re-edit the arrangements. If I don't like the way a song is laid out, I don't buy it in the first place. Not all Live DJs agree though of course, and that's fine too, there's room for us all to do things our own way.

I think the days where laptop DJs need to worry about the 'checking your email' syndrome are coming to an end. As more and more DJs realize the power of Live as a DJ tool, and start getting out there using it, the crowds will remember that DJing is not a visual art, but an audible one. They'll remember to dance, not watch :) '

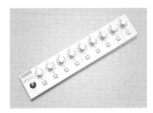

Kenton Killamix Mini

Manage your song folders

Try to come up with a system that will help you find the right track at the right time, especially if you've got a hard drive that contains thousands of songs. Classify them by genre, bpm, whatever you like. Remember you can use the Browser's search function to locate a specific tune or artist.

You can create and manage folders and move or delete their contents from within Live's browser, using the context menu – ctrl click.

If you like to use iTunes to organise your songs, create a File Browser shortcut to your iTunes Music folder.

Pre analysis

You can use the context menu in the file browser to prepare songs for importing, by pre-analysing them. You know when you import a song or audio sample into Live, and you have to wait while Live draws the waveform and calculates the original bpm? This function does this in advance, on a folder-at-a-time basis, so there's no hold-up when you want to drop a song into your Live set. Perfect for DJs who like to browse through their collection rather than have it all mapped in advance. Just locate the folder containing the songs you want to preanalyse, control-click on it, and you'll see a progress bar at the bottom, as each song is processed in turn. It can take a little while if you have a lot of songs in the folder, but it's more important to save the time for later.

Info – DJing with MP3s

Tempting though it may be to DJ with MP3s, because they're so readily available, and because they use very little disk space... don't do it. You can hear the difference. Even if you can't hear the difference at home, you'll hear it when you're running through a sound system. Ableton Live can import MP3s, sure, but I really wouldn't recommend doing a set with them, and there's not much you can do to improve the quality.

Warping entire songs

If you want total freedom to manipulate songs in Live, you have to warp them. If the warp button is off, Live won't do anything to the songs, they'll just play back at their original tempo and pitch, regardless of your Live project tempo. Some DJs do work like this, it's perfectly valid, though not very adventurous.

If you DO want to warp entire songs, Complex warp mode was designed for this purpose – for working with an entire song in a single audio clip, rather than – say – just bass or vocals or drums. Use Complex mode sparingly though, because it is a processor-hungry feature – watch that CPU meter go up!

Tap tempo

If you're working with a laptop and Live alongside a record deck, or you're crossfading in from another DJ or Live set, use tap tempo to match their bpm. Enter Midi Map Mode or Key Map Mode and assign a MIDI control or qwerty character to this function. Start tapping away. Live assumes that you're tapping in fours, and will keep updating the bpm constantly, as long as you keep tapping.

Opinion

Is it cheating to have an entire song on one Live clip, as some DJs do? No.

Live DJing with John 00 Fleming

'The main thing is that it completely reinvents the role of the DJ; we can perform live remixes and bootlegs on the dance floor; we can reconstruct any track the way we want it to happen, making our sets completely unique. Also, having your whole music collection with you on a tiny hard drive makes complete sense. Gone are the days of lugging around heavy record boxes; I don't understand DJs that still do this.

For hardware control I use the Evolution uc33, because it's like a mini mixing desk. The way I use Ableton (in performance) is how I work in the recording studio; to have as much control as possible is vital for me. There are many controllers around that are DJ based, they simply don't have enough control for me. I mix multiple tracks at the same time, loaded with effects!

I've just started using Echo Audio's Indigo DJ, because it's one less thing to plug in when you get to a gig. This simply slots into the laptop giving me 2 x stereo outputs. Seems to be perfect for the job in hand, I'm very pleased with it.

I use ReWire in the recording studio, but am not keen to use this in a club. The concept is a great one, but I've only just got to trust the new generation of laptops and operating systems, knowing that they wont crash on me. ReWire for me represents a disaster waiting to happen. When a crash happens in a club, it can seem to take forever to restart that computer...thankfully those days are over.'

The Indigo audio card

Studio notes

When I say 'studio', I'm basically talking about anything that isn't to do with performance; especially things which happen in the Arrangement View – songwriting, production, remixes. As usual, refer to all other chapters in this book – the regular Live crossover warnings apply! These are just some brief random notes relating to 'the studio' that don't fit anywhere else...

If you spend a lot of time in the Arrangement View, maybe you should be using Live's Locators; markers which allow you to jump around your song's timeline. There are little buttons for previous, set, and next locator. You can click anywhere in the timeline and create a locator. You can create locators while Live is playing. Even better, the locator set, previous, and next buttons are midi and keyboard assignable, so you can use a MIDI controller to navigate the timeline. Cmd – r on a locator to name it.

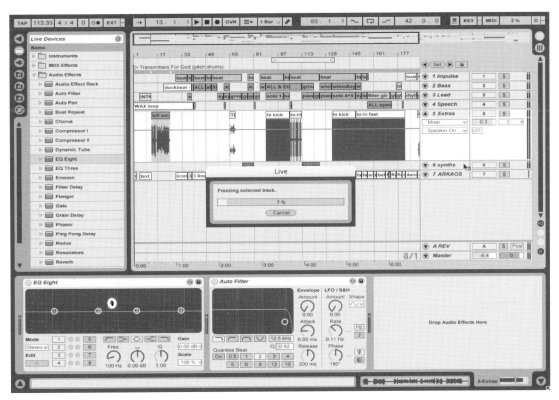

Track freeze in progress

Track Freeze is something that might be familiar to users of other DAWs. It's used to cut the CPU load arising from effects and software instruments. Select 'Freeze Track' from the Edit menu, or use the ever-present context menu, and a temporary audio reference file is created for every clip in the track. Until the track is unfrozen, Live uses the reference files instead of the devices in the track. This works very well – if you're having any playback problems, or you're trying to run a Live set created on a more powerful computer, try it.

- Frozen plug-in tracks can be played on computers that don't have the original plug-in.
- Mixer functions are still available for frozen tracks.

Track delay in Session View

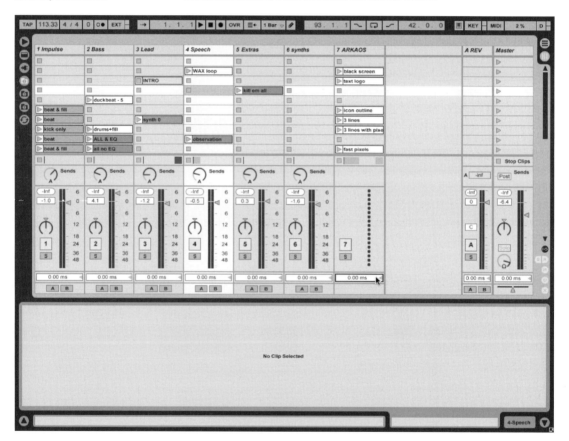

Choose Track Delay from the View menu (in either Arrangement or Session Views) and a small box appears in the mixer section for each track in your set, displaying '0.00 ms'. Click and drag in this field to introduce track delay. A higher value 'moves' the track later (in comparison with the song), while a minus value will cause the track to start playing earlier; values of plus/minus one second are possible.

- Track Delay won't work unless you've selected 'Options/Delay Compensation'.

Click above the Arrangement View's track area – this is the Scrub Area – and playback will jump to that point, according to your global quantization setting. If you click and hold, playback will loop, again, according to global quantization. If global quantization is off altogether, or very small, you can click and drag in the scrub area and hear your progress as you 'scrub' through – a term familiar to video editors.

- You can scrub in clips too (warping has to be on).
- You can't automate anything in the Scrub Area!
- See the ReWire coverage in Chapter 15.

See Chapter 7 for more Arrangement fun.

Songwriting

Live is a great tool for songwriting – although it may not look like it. With Live you can take a piece of music from the smallest germ of an idea to the finished overblown final production ('overblown' part optional). If you have a background of working with songwriting in a linear context, don't think you have to abandon it all in favour of loop-based music; instead enjoy the opportunities available – you can combine the best of both worlds. I know some people who have had problems making the adjustment to songwriting in Live, but it really isn't that different, and it's much more intuitive to work with song structures in Live than in Logic, for example.

If you need a beat to work over, just drag something in from the Browser, or create a MIDI clip, drop in Impulse, and create your own drum part. While these beats are looping, start working with some MIDI clips – draw in, or input from a keyboard – then go through your sample library for other sounds that might fit. Record a live instrument or voice and throw that in the mix. The great thing with Live is that you don't have to stop playback, you can just keep building the layers, and, as you create more clips, you can start moving and copying them, trying out new structures while the clips are still playing.

When I'm writing songs in Live, there's always one sound that kicks it all off – even if I come to it with a melodic idea, it doesn't really start working until a certain sound appears, whatever it might be. Live has so many alleyways you can get lost in, but as you understand it better, it starts working for you – you're not just following the software anymore. If you've got any old songs that you put on ice because they weren't getting anywhere, throw them into Live and see what happens – it can help you see your songs from different perspectives; Live makes it easy to import existing parts, and of course to manipulate them freely – it can help you isolate the germ that made your song work in the first place, and put it in a different (hopefully better) setting. This re-use of old material crosses into the jamming/remix/mashup philosophies that Live embraces.

- Songs made in Live don't have to be loop-based, they don't have to be 'dance' music, they don't have to sound 'electronic'... and they don't have be in 4/4 time.

Jen Bloom is a singer/songwriter/pianist from New York, who has recently started to use Live:

Quote

'Before Live came along, I was recording my songs on a lovely Radio Shack mono crap recorder. Then my brother recorded songs we did together on Acid and Audacity. Live is great for me because I love experimenting with sound, and the multiple uses Live offers... and the user-friendly tutorials for girls like me who have no idea what they're doing!

Live is the first program which has gotten me psyched enough to actually jump into computer music, a previously daunting task. I don't yet use Live's software instruments, but I will get to it. I also plan to run Live onstage alongside my other instruments.' – *Jen Bloom*

Info – toomuchchoiceitis

Live has a relatively simple interface, but it's still easy to lose your perspective – too much choice! If you're starting to feel blocked, give yourself some limitations to work against. For example I had a song I was struggling to finish, it had 8 or 9 tracks, with drums, percussion, various synths and basses. All the parts worked individually, but somehow they didn't hang together as a song. Rather than delete any parts or change the basic structure, I made a rule: only four tracks could be playing at any time, so the tracks would have to 'take turns'. It worked great – cleared the air a little bit. Cutting things down is nearly always a good idea – I'm quite ruthless when working on remixes; you start rooting around in a track and you find things that don't need to be there. Live's Arrangement View makes it a snap to do things like this, using a combination of actions such as splitting clips, and automation track activation/deactivation. Make your own rules – they could apply to effects, or the number of scenes or clips...whatever it takes.

(Below) A mashup in progress in Session View

(Opposite page) two mashups in Arrangement View

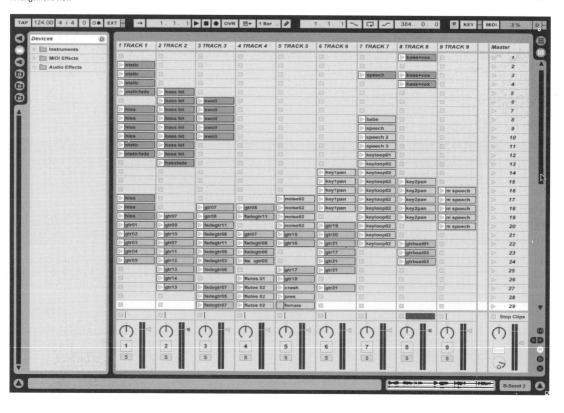

Chapter 12: Studio notes

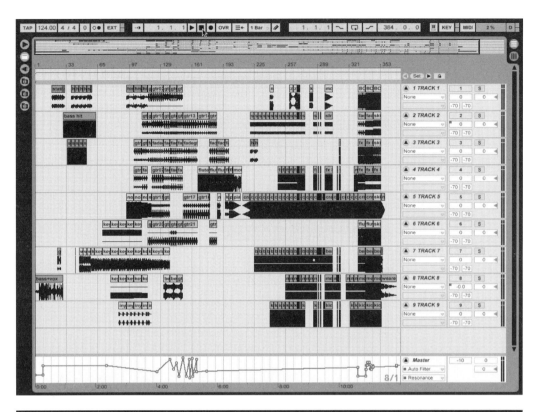

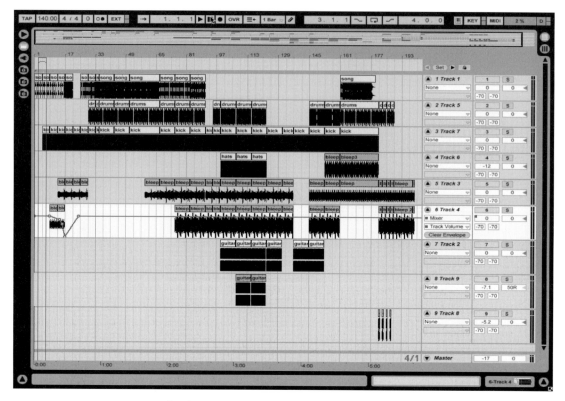

Another mashup in Arrangement View

Remixes and mashups with Live

Live is the ultimate remix/mashup tool, taking away the torture involved in all that slicing and rearranging. There were times when certain decisions were based on wanting to get it over with, rather than what would sound good. Tempo manipulation used be the worst thing about remixing – it was time-consuming, and changes to a song's original tempo were restricted to a narrow range. Live has made this process relatively invisible, and the Auto-Warp feature is the icing on the cake. It's just too easy! It's cheating! Then once everything is locked into time, you can add as much other stuff as you want – how about more audio clips, or software instrument parts? Resample sections and re-process them; whatever gets the job done.

Remixing and mashups are where DJing and 'musicianship' meet – Live makes it so easy to drop parts of other people's songs into your own – or to drop your own sounds into other people's songs. For one mashup I did of two 1970s songs, I recorded myself singing and playing bass through the mic of my laptop, and used that in the intro. Throughout the song I added some speech from a TV documentary, and some other sounds that I recorded on minidisc a year or two earlier (in my live set, I have drums from 8-track cassette demos I made 15 years ago – and they sound great – hissy, but great).

These are the mashup baby steps:

(Opposite page) Auto warping – in progress and (lower pic) Auto warping completed

- Find two songs you want to work with. Live makes it easy to fit anything to almost anything else, but you still have to apply some good taste!

Chapter 12: Studio notes

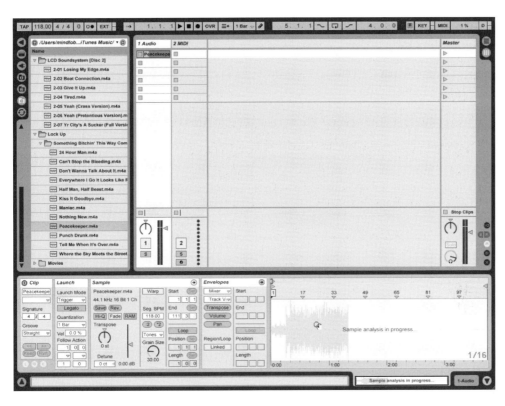

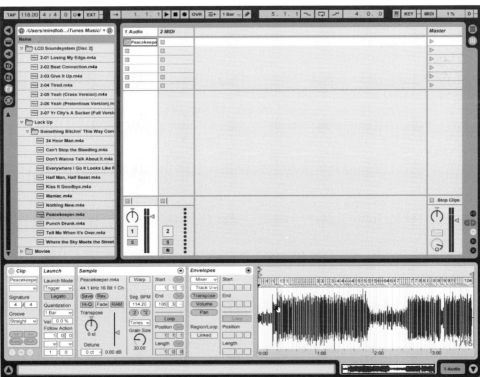

- Load and Auto-Warp the songs to adjoining audio tracks (in the Session View). Although you can use MP3s, the finished mix will sound better if you use full quality AIFs or WAVs.

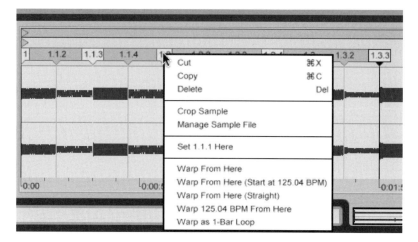

The context menu warp options

- Check both songs have warped correctly; sometimes the intros need looking at.
- Go through the songs and find the sections you want to use. Isolate the sections into separate clips. Define the start and end points of the sections (they're probably going to be loops).
- Remember that Live can zoom right in for finer cuts, if you want to make very small slices.
- Consolidate the clips, to trim away the junk (this will necessitate a quick detour to the Arrangement View).
- Choose the best-sounding warp modes for your clips – do this on an individual basis. Sometimes the 'right' warp mode isn't the 'best'.
- You might need to adjust the volumes of the various clips – I use the clip gain sliders for this, so it doesn't interfere with anything i might do at track level.
- Structure the mashup as you see fit. It can be clever, or groovy, or funny, or totally destructive – you are in control.
- When you're done, record it into the Arrangement View; if inspiration strikes during the recording process and it takes you off on a tangent – go with it.
- Mix the finished mashup to a stereo master, then hide from the authorities! Of course these projects should only be undertaken for your own entertainment. the laws of copyright are very strict. Live is top dog at this – there's no competition.

Build a 16-step sequencer

If you've got a hankering for some retro-style step sequencing, but you don't have (or can't afford) the hardware, there is a way to do it in Live. This is a trick that you won't find anywhere else! Even better, unlike some of the other Live 'creations' described in this book, this one doesn't require any complicated MIDI routing, and is fully cross-platform.

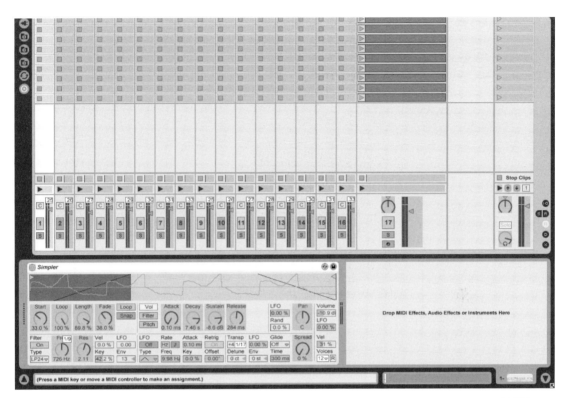

The 16-step sequencer with MIDI mapping

It started when I was reading about hardware step sequencers, and I wanted to use Live and my UC33 to emulate that experience; I came up with this solution. Here's how it works:

- Create a Live set with 17 MIDI tracks, and a return track with Ping Pong Delay.
- Load Simpler into track 1. Choose a preset with a suitable sound...bass or lead, that's your choice!
- Once you've got the Simpler sound the way you want it, save it as a preset called 'sequencer sound'.
- Now load Simpler into the next 15 tracks, and load the 'sequencer sound' preset in each.
- Track 17 is for drums – more on that later.
- Back to track 1 – create an empty 1-bar MIDI clip. Draw 16 adjoining notes of equal length, filling the bar.
- Select all of the notes except the first one, and deactivate them.
- Copy the clip across tracks 2-16, and for each track activate the next note in the row, while deactivating the previous one.
- Now you have to do some MIDI mapping. Assign the UC33's faders 1-8 to the first 8 faders in Live's mixer. Assign the first row of 8 knobs to Simpler's transpose control in each track. Assign the second row of knobs to Simpler's frequency control in each track. Assign the third row of knobs to the send knob for each track.
- For tracks 9-16, you'll need to create a UC33 preset that sends on

Info

Step sequencers were the first sequencers around, in the days of hardware; using a deceptively simple structure – playing 16 (typically) notes, one after the other, in an endless loop, with parameters such as pitch being editable in real-time. It's amazing how much can be achieved with this simple arrangement. For modern hardware equivalents, take a look at Doepfer's products.

channel 2 (use Enigma to set this up); then assign the necessary MIDI controllers for those tracks, just like tracks 1-8.
- Now, when you trigger the corresponding scene, the clips will begin playing together, but the 16 notes will play in succession, just like a step sequence! As long as your MIDI clips are set to loop, this will keep playing indefinitely, while you change the volume, pitch, frequency and fx send for each note.
- You can also use the computer keyboard to mute/solo individual tracks for more rhythmic interest.
- Assign fader 9 to song tempo.
- Load Impulse and some drum loops in track 17, and use follow actions to instigate a little random playback.
- Effects in the master track will make a lot of difference to the overall sound. To get the tone I wanted, I used (from left to right) Redux, Phaser, Saturator, and Compressor II.

Nearly everything you do with this setup sounds good... it's not exactly the same as using hardware, but it's close, and it has value in its own right. Hit record at any time and commit your sequencers to disk for later use.

This formula was created before device racks and their macros appeared on the Live scene. There may be other ways of creating a similar effect – loading several instances of Simpler into device rack chains, for example – but if you're using a UC33 to control things, this method works fine.

Who knows what other hidden 'features' await within Live? maybe you know... share them!

Movie notes

Movie soundtracks with Live

'Whenever the director makes picture changes, I will not have to make cuts anymore, but simply stretch time. We change a lot of things in the final dub. This is when the sound effects come in, sometimes the whole feel of the movie changes. This always is a great moment. It is fantastic to be able to manipulate things, to make changes at the very last moment. There is this fine line between writing and manipulating. This is an ongoing process. So, rather than delivering things in Pro Tools and doing cuts all the time, Live makes things much easier.' – Hans Zimmer

You just know Ableton are serious about something if it involves adding a new window, and Live 6 brings not one but two new windows – one for Sampler (see the 'Sampling' chapter), and one for movie playback. At long last...

People have long been using Live for movie soundtracks, thanks to ReWire technology, and applications such as ReVision and Logic, but as of Live 6, its a lot easier. Full QuickTime movie support is coming to Live – gradually.

What makes Live good for movie soundtracks? It's the warp markers, it's the ability to gently encourage (or force) pieces of audio to fit desired lengths, while working in real-time. Drag'n'drop QuickTime movies into a track in Live; process their audio, trim their start/end points, watch the video in full screen on a second display – it's getting dangerously close to video editing! This is going to introduce a horde of Live users to soundtrack work...

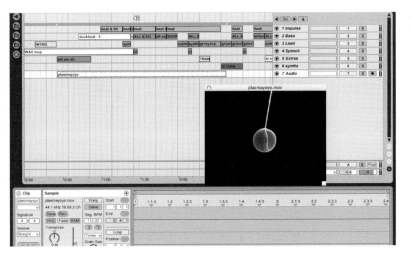

A QuickTime movie in Live's movie window

You can begin by simply dropping a QuickTime movie into Arrangement View. If you drop a movie into Session View, you'll get the audio, but no image. Any movies with a .MOV suffix should work fine. .MPGs, like the ones I get from my Sony Cybershot, will require conversion first.

Once you load the movie, a new audio track will be created, and the Video Window will open automatically. Double-click in the Video Window to jump to full-screen playback. This is a great way to work if you have a second display connected to your computer. The imported movie will appear, effectively, as a regular audio clip, though with small dots, to represent the familiar movie frame graphic. Unlike some DAWs, however, you can't zoom into the timeline and look at individual movie frames.

One more thing – QuickTime movies can contain MIDI tracks, and Live can of course contain MIDI tracks. But if you import a QuickTime movie into Live containing MIDI, forget it. The MIDI will be ignored. You'd have to use QuickTime Pro to separate the video and MIDI elements before importing.

Your imported movie's audio will play just like that of any other audio clip, and this audio can be warped, looped, processed, etc. Select your video clip, and look in the Clip View – you'll see the regular Clip, Sample, and Envelope options. You can drop in audio effect devices as usual, and the context menu (ctrl-click) reveals the usual options.

Frank Blum is a German composer who has considerable experience of using Live to score movies:

Quote

'At the moment I´m working on a few different short movies – since Live 6 it´s much easier to do. Load a QuickTime movie in one track, mark the sync points with locators and then just start trying different soft synths to get a feeling for the scene. I'm still using a lot of Reaktor synths (there are some amazing ones out there); the Miroslav Philharmonik is great for all orchestral sounds, and I have different sound libraries to load into Sampler and modify to make background textures.

Two things I´m still missing in Live: the opportunity to have Arrangement View and Session View at the same time, and a tool palette like all the other apps have, to make it easier to cut and drag files...and to have more than one automation parameter view simultaneously.' – *Frank Blum*

Info – two screens are better

If you're serious about working with video, a second display is one of the best buys you could make. Good quality LCD displays are so cheap these days. Whether you're using a laptop or a desktop computer, you'll love the extra screen space. There's no configuration for second displays, as far as Live is concerned – just double-click the Video Window to enlarge it, and drag to the other display.

You don't have to separate or otherwise extract the audio from the movie before we start work on it (in fact you can't, except by consolidating the clip). We don't even have to look at the movie if we don't want to – just close the Video Window (you can always re-open it later from the View menu).

If you activate warping for your video clip, then it will sync to the project bpm. This means that both the audio and video in the clip will speed up or slow down as required. If you want the movie and audio to maintain their original speed, disable warping...or, activate warping, and, in the box below that, activate the tempo master switch. This will enable the movie to play at it's original rate, while forcing the rest of the project to follow along. Of course, warping means that you can alter the timing of sections of the clip. You can't separate the movie from the audio – if you use warp markers to accelerate or decelerate part of the clip, the visuals will go faster/slower with the audio. Any global tempo changes will similarly affect both the audio and video in the movie clip – unless you've previously set the video clip as sync master.

You could say with video clips that you're really just working with the audio, and the movie sort of follows along. You can put multiple movies in the same track, and in different tracks. The bottom-most track will take priority, and the others will only show through 'gap's or before/after the bottom-most.

If you consolidate, reverse, or crop a video clip, the video component disappears; and – IMPORTANT – read the final step in this section before getting too excited about Live's video editing.

Locators

QuickTime markers that were inserted by other video editing applications can be viewed in Live, but not interacted with in any way. It's a primitive implementation at present, like all of Live's video features, but will hopefully lead to greater integration in future.

Live's locators can be very useful when working with movies. Use them to indicate and navigate movie scenes within the Arrangement View; give them names that will help you identify the section of the movie they refer to. See the 'Performance' and 'Studio' chapters for more on working with locators.

Exporting it all together?

What a shame we can't yet run video out from session view, so we can VJ our own live sets! If you want a 'workaround' for this, you could run a video track in the Arrangement View, while working with audio and MIDI clips in Session View at the same time; use the Arrangement Loop to loop the video if necessary. You can run the video out to a projector in exactly the same way as with a display.

This is all great, but what happens when you try to export your Live set with video? Errr…that's the not-so-good news. Any audio from your movie clips will be included with the rendered Live stereo mix as usual, but there's no way of exporting the video content – so Live is not yet able to do double-duty as a video editing product! This is one of the last hurdles that prevents Live from being considered a fully-functioning DAW…full QuickTime video export is one of the functions that still sends me back to Logic Pro at regular intervals.

However, let's look on the bright side…we can bring video into Live, those other features are bound to come soon, and for those of us who enjoy sampling from movies or TV shows, this feature significantly shortens the time it takes to get a piece of audio from a QuickTime movie into Simpler or Sampler.

ReWire Live to another DAW

This one isn't a 'cheat' or 'workround' – it's the regular way of doing it. Bite the bullet and ReWire Live to another DAW. Simple as that. Read more about ReWire in Chapter 15.

> **Info – Live's useful movie tools**
>
> What's helpful when you're using Live for movie soundtracks:
>
> Warping – stretch your audio or music to fit movie edits.
> ReWire – synchronize Live to a movie-friendly DAW, like Logic or Cubase, or to the ReVision QuickTime player.
> Locators – use Live's locators to label and jump between key movie edit points.

Teaching notes

How to get somebody hooked on Live

If you want to get somebody hooked on Live, this is what to do (they'll thank you for it later):

1. Create an empty Live set, with five audio tracks. Work in the Session View. Set global quantization to 1 Bar.
2. Put one audio effect on each track ('fun' things like delays, not 'sensible' things like EQ), and an Auto Filter on the master track.
3. Drag'n'drop four audio clips into each track, and make sure they're nice bright colours.
4. The majority of clips should be set to loop, but include a couple of one-shots.
5. Enter Key Map Mode (cmd-k), and assign a different letter of the alphabet to trigger every clip. Label each clip with the letter that triggers it.
6. Set the launch mode of all clips to 'Toggle' in the Launch box (or set 'toggle' as the default in Preferences/Defaults).
7. Choose a one-shot – preferably a speech sample – and quantize it to 1/16ths, change its launch mode to Trigger, and disable looping for that clipl.
8. Use Key Map Mode to assign letters to activate the effect on/off buttons.
9. Name each track with the letter necessary to fire that track's effect.
10. Hide the browser, in/outs, overview, sends, etc – clear the decks, and enter full screen mode (see the screen shot for a view of the overall set).

The key mapping allows beginners to get a groove going in the shortest possible time, and with the minimum of explanation. You can simply tell your students to begin pressing letters and observe what happens. Toggle Mode means you don't have to explain how to start/stop individual tracks, all they need is the spacebar to start/stop the entire set. With the one-bar global quantization, clips always come in on time, and the 1/16th quantization for selected one-shots adds that extra 'DJ scratching a record' vibe – tacky though it is, newcomers love that kind of thing, especially kids. I've used a template based on this format to introduce Live to all kinds of people – it creates a game-like environment, emphasising the fun and real-time control that Live offers. The next step is to explain more about the effects, the mixer (mainly why red level meters are a Bad Thing), tempo

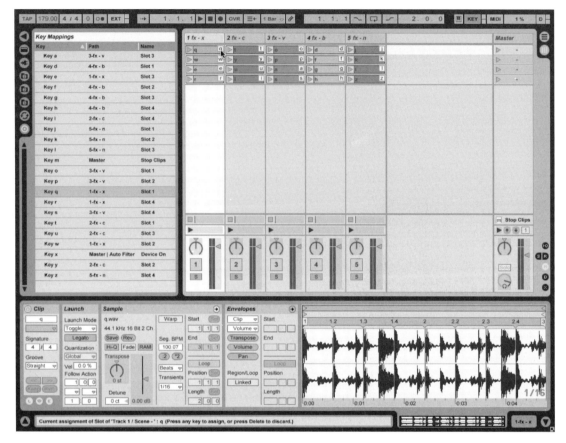

Keyboard mapping

changes, and recording what they're doing; then viewing and editing it all in the Arrangement view.

Finally, add some transposition to the 1/16th clip – as your student constantly re-triggers the speech sample, get them to move the clip's Transpose knob up and down, they'll love it.

In the classroom with Live

I've taught Live to 'regular' school kids, kids with attention problems, adults with learning difficulties, prisoners, people in drug rehab, youth centres, students at risk of dropping out of college, and patients in secure psychiatric units. Live can seem complicated, but it's really down to how you introduce it to the students; taking time to set up a good Live demo file as discussed above will make all the difference. Remember to take advantage of Live's ability to hide interface elements, so you can focus the students' attention where you want it. Even on one-day courses, I've had kids jamming with clips and effects, recording their voices, then recording it and editing automation. The real-time control wins them over, especially once they start recording their own sounds. Kids love that old-school sampling stuff like recording a beat being banged out on a plastic chair, and using warp markers to lock it to a tight rhythm.

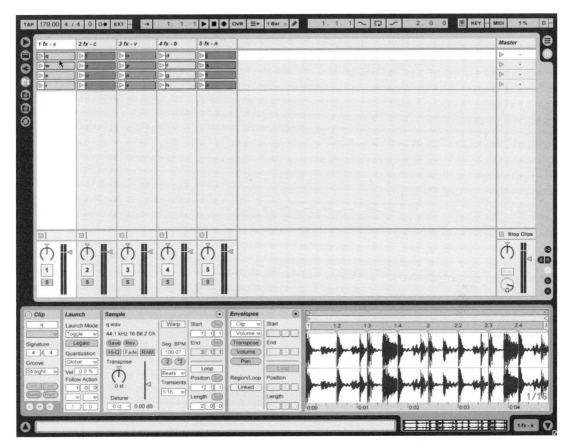

Completed set

Nothing beats Apple's GarageBand for drag'n'drop simplicity, if you want to show people how to build songs in a linear fashion, but Live has the advantage of the real-time performance elements as an attention-grabber, and then of course it goes on from there, to far deeper levels of creativity. This is also where Ableton's one-product philosophy pays off – people love to know that the friendly, colourful, software they're 'playing' with is used on stages, and in clubs, and in studios, and in movies, around the world. You might not think of yourself as a 'teacher', but with the right combination of Live knowledge, general musical experience, personality... you could have a lot to offer... and it's a two way thing; you learn a lot too.

I did a project recently where we had groups of kids in 4-day blocks. The kids worked in pairs, spending the first 2 days creating a song in Live, and the second 2 days remixing it. This gave us a chance to do things like working with tempo changes, and bouncing down 4-bar chunks of the original mix to a single track, then looping and mangling it. They also experimented with envelopes – drawing curves in empty tracks, and then pasting them onto parameters in other tracks (volume, tempo, effects levels, cut-off, etc), and listening to the quite random results. Quite 'conceptual', but also fun – and some great sounds came from it.

During another recent project, one of the 11-year olds mentioned that he could play guitar. I showed him a demo movie from the Ableton site about working with guitars, and we soon had him recording guitar loops, working with plug-ins, transposing down to create bass parts, and sharing the sounds with his fellow students: his first experience of recording guitars. It was a fantastic time in the class, with the other kids making suggestions about what he could play for them, and he was – of course – very excited and proud to be 'used' in this way.

Working in classrooms with Live will teach you more about it too, especially when you hear some of the great stuff that kids will come up with. It reminds you that there's a lot of BS around electronic music – you start to realise how much of what you hear is really the software talking; how easy it is to be average with this kind of music, and how hard it is to be really good!

At the moment, most of my teaching work is conducted on a 1-to-1 basis, with DJs and musicians. Not everybody wants to sit through a pre-structured Live course in a group, but there are a lot of people who want one-day sessions covering very specific topics, such as configuring their new hardware synth with Live, or preparing a Live set for their first gig.

Working in classrooms with Live will teach you more about it too

Using Live with other software and hardware

In general, I favour using Live on its own – bouncing its ever-expanding feature set against its limitations; however, the real world is full of reasons for Live to communicate with other music gear – maybe one application does something another doesn't, or maybe you've got a song created in Logic, and you need it to run alongside Live. On the hardware side, you may want to set Live at the heart of your studio, triggering sounds and effects on hardware synths or samplers, or syncing via MIDI Clock or MIDI Timecode to hardware recording systems. And then you may enter other realms; controlling VJ equipment, lighting rigs – anything that can be controlled with MIDI.

ReWire

ReWire was created by Propellerhead, makers of Reason, to synchronise music applications; it's become universal – all sequencers now include ReWire support. It's invisible – you don't have to buy it, or install it separately – you hardly even have to tell it to do anything. The level of integration between ReWired applications varies, from basic sync, to streaming MIDI and audio through each other's inputs/outputs. In any ReWire setup, one application takes the role of Master, the other (or others) Slave(s). These roles are dictated by a simple means – the application that's opened first is the master. Some apps play both roles equally well, others insist on being boss.

Live and Reason – somebody has to be in charge

Reason is Propellerhead's incredibly popular software studio – the one that looks like a hardware rack. Reason doesn't cut it as a standalone production centre: the interface is inefficient, and Live has superior audio facilities; Reason can't record audio – it's purely a synth and sampling system (and a sampler without recording is...well...). ReWire brings these two together, allowing you to enjoy the best of each.

ReWiring Live with Reason is easy. Launch Live first, then Reason, to establish the ReWire relationship. In Reason, create some instruments and program some parts for each. Hit the spacebar to start/stop play in either the Reason or Live window, they'll play in sync. You won't hear anything though, until you route Reason through Live's outputs. In your first available Live audio track, choose 'Reason' from the Input menu. The Input Channel slot below that should display '1/2, mix L/R', representing Reason's main stereo output. If both apps are playing, you'll see some activity on the small meter

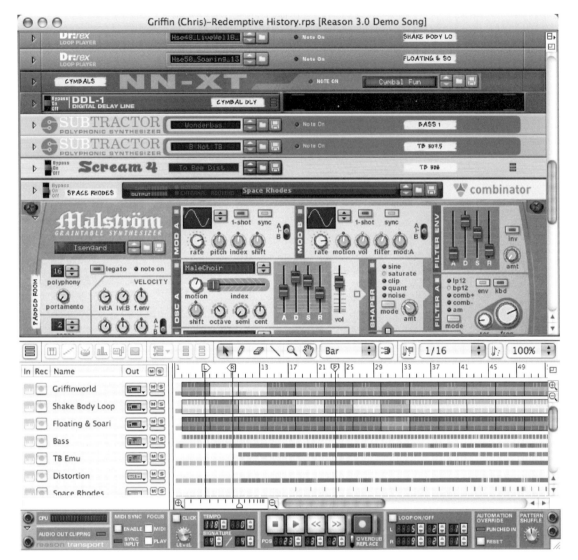

Typical Reason rack

in the Input channel slot. You still won't hear anything until you arm that Live track by clicking on the 'arm' button – it'll turn red. Now you've got Reason coming through, you can process it and record it into audio clips like anything else coming through Live.

Render without recording

It's possible to render Reason parts from Live without recording them first. Let's say you want to render 8 bars of Reason parts as part of your Live song. In the Arrangement View, click and drag to highlight the first 8 bars of the Live timeline, even though there's nothing to represent the Reason parts. Hit shift/command/r to render. Anything in your Live set is rendered, as well as the first 8 bars of your Reason song. This works even if you have no audio or MIDI content at all in Live, and are just looking at an empty Arrangement View. You can use this method to render your Reason material through Live-

Chapter 15: Using Live with other software and hardware   113

Reason outputs in Live

hosted plug-ins – you can do fun stuff by drawing in automation for effects and mixer parameters in the empty Live audio track, and then rendering the Reason output through it.

Live set sending automation to Reason

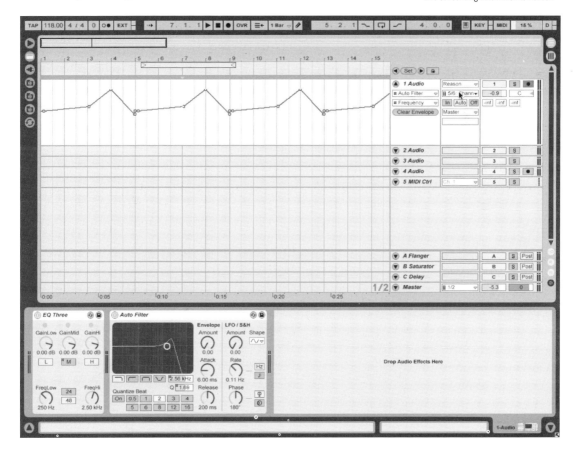

However, you'll probably want individual Reason instruments to go to separate Live tracks – click on the Reason '1/2, L/R' in the Input slot, to see a list of available Reason outputs. However, none of them will do anything, because at the moment all Reason parts are coming from the main stereo output. So, back to the Reason rack...hit 'tab' to flip the rack over. At the top, you'll see the back of the hardware interface – the only component that can't be removed from a Reason rack (by the way, when ReWire has been invoked, the front of the hardware interface says 'rewire slave mode').

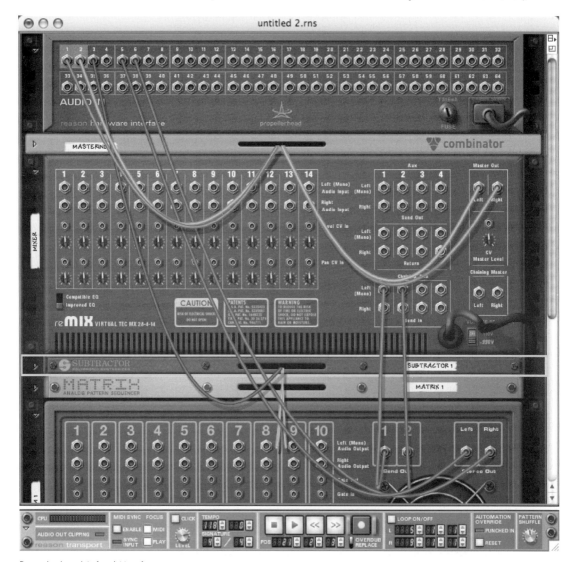

Reason hardware interface (at top of rack)

You'll notice that your mixer's left/right master outs are going to inputs 1/2 in the hardware interface – the main stereo out. Go to each Reason device, and drag its main output cables, whether mono or stereo, to separate inputs in the hardware interface. Let's say Redrum is going to 3/4, for example. Now, when you go back to Live, create a second audio track, and for that one choose 3/4,

Chapter 15: Using Live with other software and hardware   115

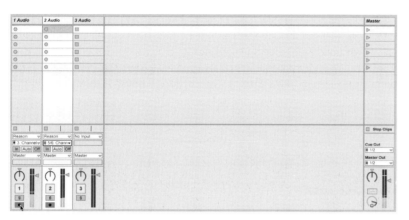

Individual Reason outputs in Live

instead of 1/2. Arm it, start playing, and you'll hear your drum track coming through separately from the rest of the Reason mix. Mute track 1 to check it! Repeat this procedure for remaining Reason parts. This gives you the ability to mix, process and record the Reason parts separately within Live. You can delete the mixer altogether if you don't think you'll need it.

Info – safety first

Although it's great to be able to render a Live/Reason song without having to record the Reason material as audio first, it's still a good idea to create AIF or WAV versions of anything you create with MIDI. Over time, your setup changes, software is updated, obsoleted...things happen, and you're unable to use that original software instrument or preset; you can't recreate the sound in your song.

Reason won't send MIDI to Live, but it works fine the other way round. Create a MIDI track in Live, and choose Reason as its Output Type. In the output chooser slot below that, you'll see a list of every device in your Reason

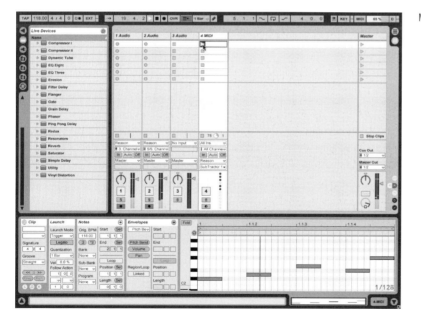

MIDI sent from Live to Reason, and

rack. Choose one, then you can send MIDI notes and controllers to Reason. Of course, you can be sending MIDI to Reason at the same time as dealing with its incoming audio on adjoining tracks.

When you've finished working with any ReWire combination, remember to quit the slave first. Well, even if you forget, it's pretty easy – Live will just refuse to go until Reason is quit first!

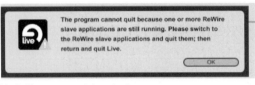
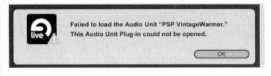

Live ReWire message and slave plug-in warning

What's the catch?

There's a price to pay when running Live as a ReWire slave. Although the Live Device plug-ins will continue to work as usual, click on the Plug-In Device Browser for third-party plug-ins and you'll be greeted by this message: 'Unfortunately, plug-ins are deactivated when running Live as a ReWire slave.' If the Live set that you're opening already contains third-party plug-ins, you'll see the following message: 'Failed to load the Audio Unit "PSP Vintage Warmer." This Audio Unit Plug-in could not be opened'.

You'll also find that Live can't access any audio ins/outs – in Audio Preferences you'll see a message saying 'Live is running in ReWire slave mode. Audio I/O is handled by the ReWire master application. Sample rate 44100 (or whatever)'.

ReWiring Live to other sequencers

Logic - selecting ReWire as input source

Logic is our example here, because it's what I use – the principles are similar with other sequencers like Cubase, though. Launch Logic first, then Live. The Live start-up window will display the following message: 'running as rewire slave'. let's say you have 3 Live audio tracks. Load a clip in each track and start them playing. In the Output slot for the first audio track, choose ReWire Out, and in the lower slot choose bus 3 (1 & 2 are for stereo output). For your second audio track repeat the procedure, choosing bus 4, and for the third track, 5. In Logic create 3 audio tracks. for Logic track 1 choose ReWire: RW Bus 3 from the channel pop-up, and repeat for the other tracks choosing Bus 4-5. This is just an example – you can also choose pairs of ReWire outputs, like Bus 3.4. You don't have to arm the Logic tracks for recording; as soon as you start a clip playing on each Live track, their output will be audible through Logic – you'll see the input levels in the meter for each track. You can then record the Live inputs, and/or apply Logic's effects. If you have a MIDI controller routed to your Live MIDI track, you should also be able to hear the output from that when you hit the pads on the Trigger Finger.

Chapter 15: Using Live with other software and hardware   117

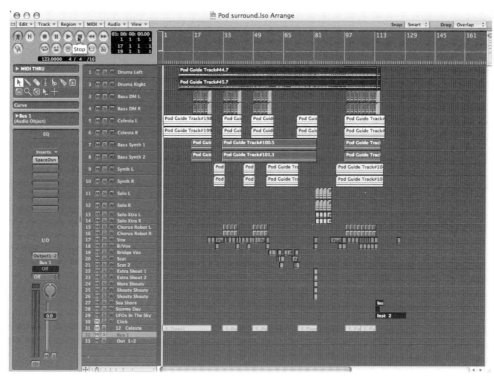

Logic general screen image and (below)
Live with Logic busses selected

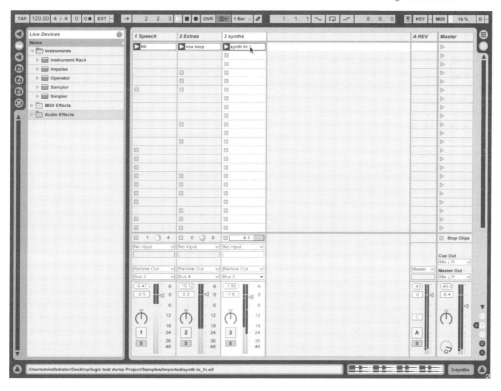

Down another Mac-only alley – ReWiring Live to GarageBand

You can ReWire Live to GarageBand; the question isn't 'how?', but 'why?'. It's a sync-only thing, with GarageBand as master; there's no way to route audio between them, but when you render your GarageBand mix, your Live parts are included. No set-up necessary, just launch GarageBand, then launch Live.

If you consider that GarageBand songs are Logic-compatible, then maybe there's something in it; you could create a quick GarageBand/Live project, then move the GarageBand portion to Logic for more 'professional' attention, and an open flow of audio and MIDI between the two. Yeah, that must be it!

There's a free Audio Unit called MidiO, which allows GarageBand to send MIDI to other applications. This works alongside ReWire to add another dimension to our unholy union. Launch GarageBand, then Live. Create a soft-

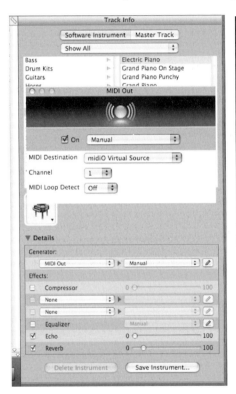

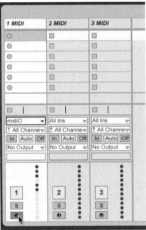

GarageBand 'export to iTunes' mixing option

(Left) MidiO in GarageBand

(Above) MidiO input in Live

ware instrument track in GarageBand, and click on the icon for the instrument. A window opens where you can select MIDI Out as the generator. Click the 'details' triangle if this option isn't showing, it's in the lower portion of the window. Click on the pencil box on the right to open another small window. Choose 'MIDI loop detect' ON and close the window. Record some notes, or import a software instrument Apple Loop. Deselect the GarageBand track to avoid creating a MIDI loop.

Now go to Live, create a MIDI track, and load Operator. Select a groovy preset. From the track's input slot, choose MIDI Out, then arm the track. Start GarageBand, and you should hear Operator playing the notes from GarageBand. You could use this to record GarageBand MIDI parts into Live, or to record audio from the GarageBand MIDI part by routing the output from the Live MIDI track to another Live audio track and recording it. Perverse as this seems, you can bet there's somebody out there doing it!

Arkaos VJ

VJing is the art of creating real-time video mixes in venues where bands or DJs are at play, and Arkaos VJ is one of the best VJ applications around. It's cross-platform, MIDI and ReWire friendly, and works well with Live; you can play a Live set and run synced visuals from your computer at the same time.

General view of Arkaos interface

Obviously, state-of-the-art computers are preferred for this, but with care you can do it on more humble systems – don't run too many tracks or plug-ins in Live, and keep your movie sizes down. Download the Arkaos VJ demo and try it. Here's how it works...

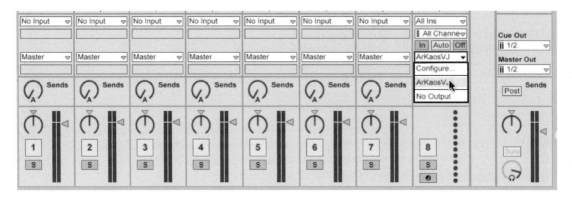

Arkaos as ReWire destination in Live

MIDI notes being sent from Live to Arkaos

Let's assume you have a LIve set ready to go, with audio or MIDI clips in the Session View. Create a new MIDI track, and name it 'Arkaos'. Launch Arkaos. Select Arkaos as an output destination in the slot at the bottom of the Live MIDI track. Live communicates with Arkaos via ReWire; it'll send MIDI only – there's no way to send audio to Arkaos. Now create MIDI clips as usual, sending notes to Arkaos as if it was a software instrument within Live; the only difference is that these notes trigger images, not sounds. You can even use Live's clip automation to send MIDI controllers to Arkaos' effects. Arkaos VJ doesn't have MIDI learn, so you'll have to enter controller numbers for each parameter; a slow process if

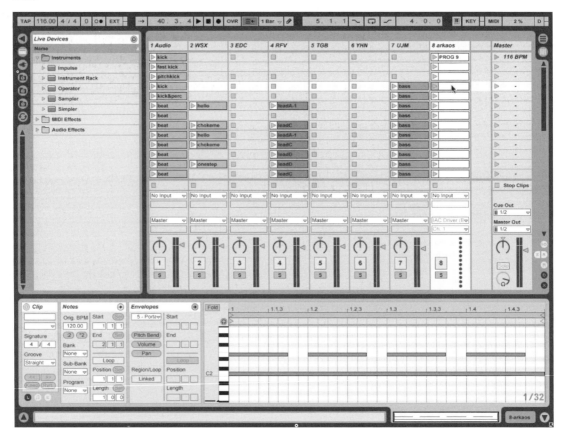

you're using a lot of images, but the results are worth it – close integration between your music and visuals.

Click on the MIDI keyboard at the bottom left of the Arkaos patch window to see the 'virtual keyboard' that corresponds to the vertical 'piano roll' keyboard in Live's MIDI Note Editor. Drag'n'drop your images in position, draw in the appropriate notes in Live, and hit play; Arkaos will begin to do its thing.

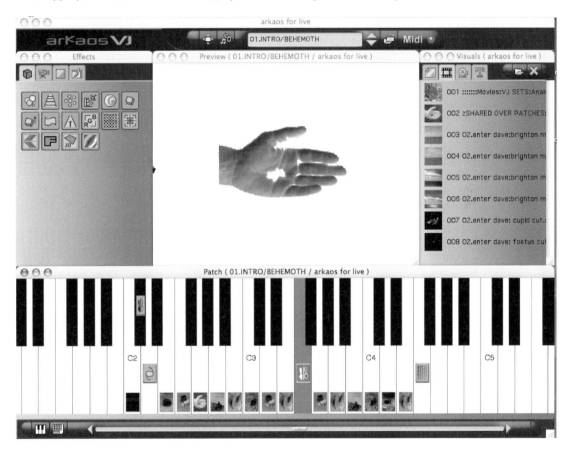

Arkaos with 'virtual keyboard'

Experimentation is rewarded: different note lengths will cause movies to play for more or less of their entirety. A Live MIDI clip can send a program change – the Program Change Select box is in the 'Notes' box in the Clip View – and you can use these to load the next Arkaos patch; I use a separate patch for each song. Rename the MIDI clips in the Live 'Arkaos' track to help you identify them quickly. There's no reason why you can't run Live in full screen and obscure Arkaos completely, it'll still feed your video projector as long as you've got display mirroring turned off. However, I like to close all other Arkaos windows, shrink the preview window down small, then stick it in the top right of my screen. I drag Live's window out as large as possible, without entering full screen or obscuring the Arkaos preview.

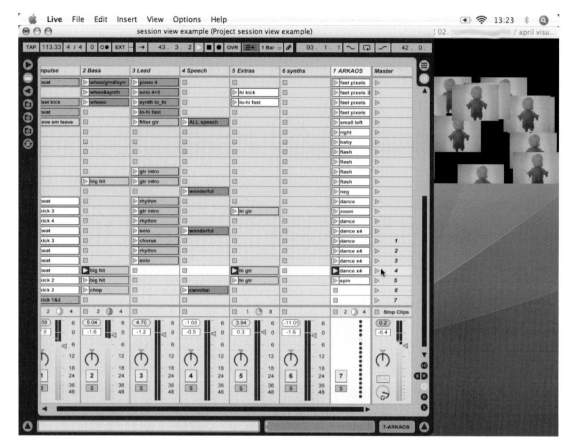

Live and Arkaos together for performance use

It's fascinating to compose with music and video at the same time. After a while the boundaries disappear, and you become a true A/V superstar!

MIDI Time Code and MIDI Clock

Live can send or receive MIDI Time Code (MTC) and MIDI clock. Very useful for communicating with MIDI-compatible hardware devices, such as sequencers, synths, samplers, grooveboxes, and lighting systems. Using Live with an external hardware device, such as a synth or sampler or sound module, is pretty much like ReWiring it to other software. Most of your setup time will be spent rooting around in the manual for the hardware in question; as usual there are few complications to deal with at the Live end. A common cause of problems is channel numbers – make sure both devices are on the same channel, ie 1, or choose 'omni' mode, which means the devices will look for MIDI on all channels. Live's MIDI clips can send MIDI controllers (CCs), bank changes, or program changes, so you can send MIDI to other applications and hardware with exactly the regular Live freedom.

Live's ability to send MIDI can come in handy even in simple situations, for example I use it to send MIDI Clock to a Boss GT-6B bass effects processor, to keep the bass delay effects in sync with my Live set. I've also sent MIDI to the GT-6B via an M-Audio FW410, and an Edirol FA-66 without any problems. Just watch those channel numbers!

Using Live with hardware keyboards and controllers

A hardware controller is a device with a keyboard, and/or knobs and faders, that sends MIDI messages to your music software. Pretty much any MIDI hardware controller that's designed to work with a computer these days will have a USB connection, which is good because it's simple – like plugging in a printer or scanner – and the controller can draw power from the computer instead of using a dedicated power supply. Some controllers double as audio interfaces – containing necessary sockets for microphones and instruments; these often connect via FireWire or USB2 rather than regular USB. With Live, MIDI messages from these units can be used to control track volume and panning, effects levels, transport, clip/scene/track selection, and – of course – to trigger actual musical notes or samples.

Info – best of both worlds

There's no substitute for going on stage with a Live-equipped laptop and a MIDI hardware controller. And there's no substitute for going on stage with a Live-equipped laptop and nothing else. A contradiction? Both are valid, and it's interesting to vary your approach occasionally.

Everybody who uses Live dabbles with hardware controllers at some time; it's common to end up with a collection of the things. Let's have a look at a selection of hardware – some keyboards, some controllers, some with audio interfaces – and see what each brings to its partnership with Live.

Less is more – the Kenton Killamix Mini

The Killamix is a very small USB-MIDI hardware controller. Imagine a channel strip from a larger mixer-style controller, and imagine it made of aluminium instead of the usual plastic construction. I should declare an interest here, because I designed this thing (and John Price at Kenton Electronics has taken it to another level with his input regarding multifunction buttons). The KMX, as it's known for short, has 9 knobs, 9 buttons, and a tiny joystick. The knobs are each surrounded by a ring of LEDs, and the buttons are lit (sometimes). All of these controls send preconfigured MIDI controllers, there's no software editor, and no drivers.

That's it, in terms of hardware, but the KMX has hidden functionality. Each of the knobs has a push-button feature. A push of knob 1, for example, will have the KMX sending on MIDI channel 1. Push 2, and it'll send on 2, and so on. Push 1 and 9 simultaneously, and you'll be on channel 10...get the idea? This channel change also applies to the buttons and joystick, so effectively you can use these channel changes as preset changes, giving you 16x9 knobs, 16x9 buttons, and 16 joysticks. Of course, whenever you change channels, the LEDs around the knobs update to their last positions on that channel. This is very handy visual reference, especially when you're working on a murky stage or in a darkened DJ booth.

In Live you might use the knobs for mixer faders, and the buttons for firing tracks, activating effects, whatever. The joystick is great for transposition, and of course classic functions like filtering.

The KMX is upgradeable via sysex messages from your computer, and Kenton are likely to introduce new features on an ongoing basis.

I've been using the KMX since prototype stages, and I'm glad to say the design holds up. It's not cheap by any means, but it is unique, tough, compact, and very functional – you get what you pay for.

Info – Take-over Mode

Another mapping-relevant feature from Live's preferences is Take-Over Mode. Located in the MIDI/Sync tab in Live's preferences, the Take-Over Mode pop-up lets you choose from three types of behaviour, relating to how Live 'picks up' incoming instructions from a hardware MIDI controller. Select 'None' if you simply want incoming MIDI CCs to be 'jumped to' immediately, without any polite introductions. This can be a problem for some controls...like if you grab a fader and you want to bring it smoothly up, and instead you get a sudden jump in volume. 'Pickup' will make the software wait until the hardware control passes through the software control's current value. This avoids any noticeable jumps, but means a longer wait before there's an audible response to your hardware movement. The third option, 'Value Scaling', is a compromise between the two previous options – a meeting in the middle, as one meets the other.

M-Audio Trigger Finger

The Trigger Finger is a USB MIDI controller for people who can't play keyboards – DJs, drummers...me. Instead of the usual 25/37/49/61/88 black and white 'proper' keyboard keys, it has 16 black rubber pads (yep, it's a lot like a USB version of Akai's ancient-but-still-popular MPC percussion sampler, the machine hip-hop was built on) – velocity and pressure sensitive – arranged in a neat grid, and 4 faders and 8 knobs. The Trigger Finger is powered via USB or an optional DC power supply, and also has a MIDI out connection. No drivers are required for Mac OSX or XP, and a free version of Live – Ableton Live Lite – is included, which although limited compared to the 'real' thing, is still a fine introduction to our favourite software (oops, we already have it!). The Trigger Finger has a threaded hole in the bottom for mic stand mounting. This is a great way to use it – the threaded hole is positioned off centre to the unit's body, centred instead on the rubber pads (which makes sense when you think about it). Don't hit it too hard though!

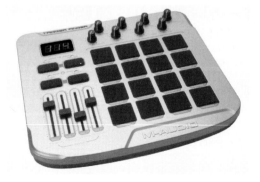
Trigger Finger

Each pad is fully assignable – for different notes, channels, and velocity options; they can also send program and bank changes. There's also an assignable pressure parameter for each pad, which corresponds to aftertouch on a keyboard; possibly good for things like effects wet/dry levels. Pressure can be disabled, or you can go the other way, and send pressure only, without any notes. A note mute feature allows you to assign the pressure parameter on the pad without confusing software that's working in 'learn' mode (like Live) – otherwise the software will receive and respond to the note being sent and not the pressure. Sure you can use the Trigger Finger with Live to create percussion patterns, but Live's flexible MIDI assignment combines with the TF's programmability to do...just about anything. Because the TF is Enigma-compatible, you don't have to worry about which of your crazy set-ups to save; you can save them all! Of course Enigma makes it much easier to create those crazy set-ups in the first place, working on your computer screen instead of trying to program anything using the TF's buttons.

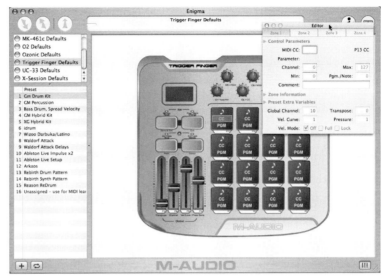

Trigger Finger in Enigma software

The Trigger Finger can store 16 presets internally. The factory default presets include two that are Live-specific – 10, which is for two Impulses on different MIDI channels, and 11, which is a general Live setup. It has to be said though, that these presets don't do anything that you couldn't achieve yourself. Preset 16 is interesting though – it's mapped to play notes from C1 to D#2, giving an unusual synth playing experience.

If you feel like a phoney, standing on stage with a keyboard, give the Trigger Finger a try. On one hand you can play logical games with it, finding correlations between Live's Session View grid, and the TF's pads, on the other you can enjoy the (relatively) physical action of (gently) striking drum pads! . And it's small enough to fit in your laptop bag.

Instant Mapping support for the Trigger Finger, is, as for other supported controllers, actually quite basic, and not incredibly useful. But it's there if you want it...look out for the little blue hand icon, which indicates that a particular device is Instant Mapping enabled. This means that, if you're using a relevant controller, like the Trigger Finger, as soon as you select the device on screen, some of its parameters are immediately under the control of the Trigger Finger, theoretically saving you the few seconds it would take to map these yourself. If your MIDI controller isn't on the Instant Mapping list, don't worry – it doesn't make much difference. It's so easy to configure MIDI hardware controllers with Live, as you'll discover shortly.

Behringer FCB1010 MIDI foot controller

The FCB1010 MIDI foot controller is mostly designed for guitarists who need to control MIDI-compatible effects or amplifiers. However, Live users, in their

FCB1010 MIDI foot controller

quest for strange MIDI gadgets, have discovered the FCB1010, and not just for those whose hands are kept busy playing guitar or bass or keyboards or clarinet; I've heard tell of laptop DJs using these things too.

The FCB has ten patch footswitches, up/down footswitches, and two expression pedals. A small display conveys necessary information. The

Info: multiple MIDI controllers

You can use up to 6 MIDI hardware controllers at a time within Live, which may seem excessive, but really is quite reasonable. In this chapter I've talked about the Trigger Finger and the Killamix, and you might want to use them alongside a keyboard, or maybe a mixer-format controller like the Evolution UC33e (also support by Live's instant mapping). You could be using a Trigger Finger for Impulse, a UC33 for general mixer duties, a Remote 25 for Operator...nice! Setting them up is easy – just choose them from the pop-ups in the Live preferences MIDI/Sync tab, as described earlier. Depending on how you're working with them, you may need to watch out for controller/channel conflicts – try setting the global channel for each controller to a different number. Notice also the context menu when you ctrl-click on a Live device: 'Lock to Control Surface 1-6'. This will keep your chosen controller focused on this device, and override any instant mapping activity (where Live automatically updates control assignments to the currently highlighted device). Remember you can assign one MIDI or QWERTY command to several different functions!

footswitches correspond to ten banks, each with ten patches – so you get up to 100 patches. It's mains powered, but no wall-wart – good news. Because it's not specifically a 'computer' audio product, MIDI out is via a regular MIDI plug, so you need to get yourself a UM-1X or UNO MIDI/USB adaptor.

Info – make some new friends

Before we go any further with this, be warned – the FCB manual needs work. What you must do – and what I did – is join the Yahoo group for FCB1010 users. Most of their posts are specific to guitar effects and amplifiers – there's little information on using Live in particular – but they know everything that you could possibly need to know about the FCB1010. There's a vast amount of information available through this group, including downloadable documents, links to software editors for PC and Mac, and firmware updates.

Any Live user could get something out of using the FCB – obviously it's relevant if your hands are busy gripping a bass or whatever, but also if you're a laptop-only performer who finds that two hands aren't enough. As usual, the only limit is your imagination. Live users have a distinct advantage with this thing, because a lot of the programming issues that drive FCB users nuts are dealt with at the Live end of things; this also helps to avoid a lot of the issues with the manual (the things that you will most likely need, like assigning MIDI notes to pedals, and copying presets, are – fortunately – described clearly enough).

The FCB1010 sends MIDI notes, CCs, and program changes, so all of the usual Live functions can be controlled – use the footswitches for transport, scrolling, scene selection, effects, and so forth. One thing to remember is that MIDI notes are actually sent with a preset; you must send a preset to send a note! Once you remember that, it's quite simple. The expression pedals are fun – you can assign them to volume, pan, filters, effect wet/dry mixes – even song tempo, which is quite perverse because it's very difficult to control in fine increments! You can specify the notes sent by the switches, so you can even use it to play notes in Operator, for that 1970s Moog Taurus vibe. If you try my MIDI setup clip idea (see 'Live Talks To Itself'!), you can use the FCB to summon a whole new mixer setup in-between or during songs. The FCB1010 can use different channel numbers for different commands, ie channel 1 for MIDI notes, and channel 2 MIDI CCs, but unfortunately the banks and patches can't store different channel numbers – it would be nice to be able to send channel 1 from bank 1, channel 2 from bank 2, etc; apparently MIDI routing utilities such as ControlAid and MIDI Ox can add a lot of extra functionality to the FCB1010.

The FCB1010 is an ideal control choice for Live-using instrumentalists and vocalists. For non-instrumentalists who want something other than a keyboard to work with, it's an unusual option, but one that keeps your hands free so you can do even more.

Jesse Terry uses the FCB1010 on stage:

Quote – Jesse Terry

I use a guitar with a MIDI pickup, going into ControlAid, then Live & Reason. I use one expression pedal to scroll between tracks (3 keyboards, 2 guitar, 1 bass and 1 with program change MIDI clips going to my Line 6 Pod XT box), and Control Aid routes the 10 buttons on my FCB 1010 to whichever track I am in.

Jesse also told me about something he used in a previous band; Circular Logic's InTime – software which enables applications such as Live to sync to real-time input from a drummer or percussionist – like an ongoing tap tempo function. This is a role reversal if ever there was one – instead of following a click in his headphones, the drummer is telling the computer what to do! This has great potential if you want to use Live in a band situation – of course you'll some sort of MIDI pads or MIDI triggers for acoustic drums.

Mackie Control Universal

Live includes out-of-the-box support for the Mackie Control Universal, which offers a unique advantage over using Live with regular MIDI hardware controls – the MCU and Live can enjoy a caring, sharing, two way relationship; any changes made on one are immediately reflected in the other. The Control is just that though – a controller; you still need an audio interface. It's also not particularly portable – more of a studio than performance item. MCU-compatibility has become a standard, though, and there are other devices

MCU Controller

which take advantage of the MCU's communication skills, while adding that audio functionality – including the Yamaha O1x, and, recently, the M-Audio ProjectMix IO. These 'newcomers' use FireWire to connect to computers, and include audio interfaces, becoming true 'all-in-one' solutions (and the ProjectMix features Pro Tools MP compatibility). Any of these units will help you keep your eyes and hands off the computer – if that matters to you.

Info – limiting the range of knobs, wheels, and faders

Live allows us to restrict the effective range of a hardware control, so for example a fader will only go from -inf dB to 0.00 dB, instead of from -inf dB to 6.00 dB as usual. I use this feature to save me from myself – from accidentally pushing a fader too far during a Live set, for example. The controls for ths used to appear in the status bar at the bottom of the Live screen, when in MIDI Map Mode, but now these tasks are performed in Live's Mapping Browser, which is available whenever you're in MIDI Map Mode. A list of mapped controllers appears, and you can type minimum and maximum values in the boxes at the right-hand side. The Mapping Browser gives you a handy overview of all your mapped MIDI controls, in case you're running into multiple-mapping confusion. While we're talking about the Mapping Browser, yes, you can also view your QWERTY computer keyboard mappings here. Just enter Key Map Mode instead of MIDI Map Mode, and all will be revealed.

M-Audio Ozonic

The Ozonic combines a 37-note keyboard, faders, knobs, and buttons, joystick, and transport controls, all connected to your computer with one FireWire cable. The top panel hosts an array of level-related controls, allowing the mixing of the Ozonic's two output pairs, and monitoring controls for input sources; DJ cueing/pre listening can be set up just as easily as monitoring for recording. Round back is a single FireWire port, MIDI in/out ports, sustain/expression pedal outputs, 4 analog jack outputs, a headphone output, and 4 analog jack inputs – one is a mic input with phantom power.

M-Audio Ozonic

The Ozonic takes the 'use Live without looking at the screen concept' quite a long way. Your computer screen can take a little bit of a back seat when you use this thing. If you really work with it, it does start to feel like you're using a keyboard workstation. The Ozonic is well laid out – a lot of controls, but they don't feel crowded, and everything is in a logical place. As usual with M-Audio gear, all buttons, knobs, and faders are individually assignable to different MIDI channels, and this is made easier by Enigma compatibility (there are also 20 onboard preset slots).

Any all-in-one unit makes certain compromises; the Ozonic has relatively few audio inputs and outputs. For maximum ins/outs use a dedicated FireWire audio interface, with a separate keyboard/controller hooked up via USB. Other than that, though, it's pretty complete, and relatively portable. You probably won't be taking it to your local Coffee Republic, but it's very neatly-sized for gig use, or for taking to your friend's place for a jam.

Info – DIY template

I've already mentioned Live's extensive computer keyboard mapping. I've been trying to come up with a more-or-less standard set-up, that I can use for all of my live (small 'l') sets. Raidius make the FinalKeys – flexible plastic overlays for computer keyboards, and I've used one of these as the basis for my Live overlay. See the photo for my working layout; I've done a couple of gigs using this template, and if you're in the mood to leave your hardware at home, this might help. The only problem with an entirely 'qwerty' based system is that you can't do any incremental changes, like with knobs or faders – everything is either very ON or very OFF, so if you use 'z' to activate a delay, you're going to get the whole thing all at once when you hit 'z'. I put the wet/dry mix of my send effects at a fairly low level, and then use key mapping to bump the send knob for that effect full on. It gives me a fast effect on/off, at a workable level, and I can always use the trackpad to make finer adjustments up or down if I need to.

Jazz Mutant Lemur

Jazz Mutant's Lemur is a 12 inch touch screen control interface for music software. Originally based on OSC (Open Sound Control), regular MIDI functionality has been included, and there are Live templates available on the website. The Lemur allows you to design your own interface, based on a library of buttons, faders, etc, and connects to your computer via the ethernet port. I suggest you keep an eye on this product, it has a lot of potential – the only thing that could stop Lemur's progress is the high price.

Going wireless – the Nintendo Wii Remote Control and WiiToMidi

There's a lot of buzz surrounding the Nintendo Wii Remote Control, specifically regarding its use with bluetooth-equipped computers. Even if you're not a gamer, you can try it – the Wiimote (as it's become known) is available separately. Mike Verdone has come up with a free Mac application called WiiToMidi, which enables the Wiimote to send MIDI notes and controllers to Ableton Live (and other MIDI applications) via the OSX IAC Bus. At the time of writing the MIDI CC's used are fixed, but that isn't usually a problem when working with Live's MIDI mapping. These are the CC's currently used:

X-axis: controller 16
Y-axis: controller 17
Z-axis: controller 18
X, Y, Z velocity: controllers 28-30

Mike Verdone

Ableton Live is my application of choice, and the one I do most of my testing with. If WiiToMidi works with anything, it works with Live.

The WiiToMidi orientation mode works very well with any X-Y assignment; Auto Filter is especially nice. That, and connecting acceleration inputs to parameters in Operator is the fastest way to get started making crazy sounds. It's a nice initial 'whoa' to show people what it can do.

You might want to tighten up the range of the MIDI controllers you're using. Controlling, say, channel volume all the way from -inf to 0 db can be very drastic. Limit the range to say -20 to 0 db and the effect is less harsh (you can apply these restrictions using the MIDI Mapping Browser).

X, Y, Z position: controllers 34-36
X, Y orientation: controllers 40-41

A button sends MIDI note C-4
B button sends MIDI note D-4

The + and – buttons can control sensitivity, and the D-Pad controls smoothing frames.

Push button 1 to enter learning mode – so you can send individual controllers to Live while in MIDI Map Mode. This disables all other CC's from being output, which is essential. It's impossible to handle the Wiimote without it sending something, it's so sensitive.

WiiToMidi also supports the Nunchuk add-on controller. What's exactly the best way to use WiiToMidi with Live? At the moment, your guess is as good as mine. I guess it's more suitable for effects control than anything else...it doesn't at the moment seem to have applications for selecting and firing scenes and clips, but that depends on what Mike does next.

Wii Remote Control

WiiToMidi window

Not actually MIDI: the Griffin Technology PowerMate

These names....the KILLAmix, the POWERmate...is this some sort of heavy metal/violence theme?

If you haven't seen it, the PowerMate is basically a giant aluminium knob that plugs into your computer via USB. It performs up to six actions, and each can be assigned to a key on your computer keyboard, or a combination of key actions. The actions are turn left, turn right, click-turn left, click-turn right, click, and long click. PowerMate is also a fine piece of USB eye candy; it has a pulsing blue light in its base, which looks coooool.

Despite its cheesy title, the Griffin Technology Powermate has long fascinated Ableton Live users – surely we can do something with it? Well, the answer has always been a qualified "yes", thanks to Live's computer keyboard mapping, and to the Griffin software which allows users to configure the keyboard actions it reproduces. Excellent news comes recently, as Griffin have just introduced a software update which supports multiple Powermates...up to 127, in fact, according to the USB standard (I declare the race ON – who's going to appear on stage with 12 of these things at once?). Use the Powermate as a bare-bones controller, triggering an effect or two, or scrolling through and triggering tracks or scenes. It also stores key combinations, so you can use it to show/hide Live interface elements such as

PowerMate

Chapter 16: Using Live with hardware keyboards and controllers   131

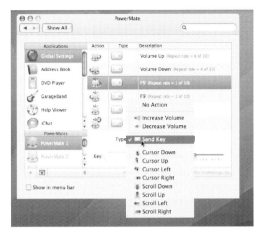

The PowerMate control panel

the mixer. You could use one for Ableton-specific functions, and a second for global, system-wide activity; you can lock a Powermate to global functions, preventing it from trying to work with the currently active application..

Live's pseudo-MIDI keyboard

There's no way to get Live's 'virtual' typing-to-MIDI keyboard to act as a remote control, it only works for sending notes to software instruments. Remember that if any function/note assignments have already been made, those notes won't be triggered by the computer keyboard. Also remember to refer to the Status Bar at the bottom of the Live screen when you're assigning MIDI parameters or using the pseudo-keyboard.

Computer keyboard input button

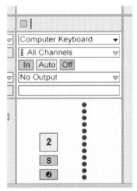

Input arming for computer keyboard

17 Using Live with audio and MIDI interfaces

If your computer has a good quality stereo audio output, there'll be a lot of times when that's enough – when you're using headphones, or hooked up to your hi-fi speakers; even playing live sometimes. Eventually though, you'll be irresistibly drawn to audio interfaces – boxes which connect to your computer, usually via FireWire or USB (USB1 or USB2, but 2 is preferable), and provide better quality inputs/outputs (and more of them), allowing you to route many tracks of audio in and out simultaneously. These interfaces range in size from small, portable units to rack mounted studio models. The smaller ones are typically bus-powered, taking their juice directly from the computer via a USB or FireWire cable. Many audio interfaces also include MIDI inputs/outputs; another dimension is added when you include MIDI controller hardware – with piano-style keys, and/or knobs, or faders, or joysticks – that also has built-in audio and MIDI interface features; see the Yamaha 01x and M-Audio Ozonic for examples of this philosophy.

Echo AudioFire 2 pocket-sized FireWire audio/MIDI interface

This is a relatively recent arrival – and it's small, very small, measuring 3.5 x 4.25 inches. Something this size isn't going to have all the bells and whistles, but it does have the essentials: 2 balanced inputs and 2 balanced outputs, 2 FireWire ports (the unit can be powered from the FireWire connection, or an included power supply), and – the highlight – a headphone output (with volume knob), independent from the main mix, which can be configured for cueing, DJ-style. MIDI and S/PDIF digital connections are available via a supplied breakout cable which connects at the rear of the unit – not too elegant for the fussy person, but keeps the size down...and those are types of connection that many people never use. The AudioFire 2 is Mac and Windows compatible, and includes drivers and a software mixer console. Usual Echo high sound quality, and strong aluminium build...brutally simple, but for me that's a good thing. I've been carrying it around for a while, and it's very unobtrusive in a laptop bag. The cueing capability and lack of XLR/phantom powered inputs make this more of a DJ device than a recording unit. It has a standalone mode, based on flash memory – just as you quit the audio console software mixer, it transmits it's settings to the AudioFire2, and these are retained, even if you power up the unit independently via a mains PSU rather than FireWire to a computer. It's a breeze to set up in Ableton Live – pair this with a Killamix Mini, and you've probably the smallest possible (but high quality) functioning DJ setup around.

Edirol FA-66 FireWire compact audio/MIDI interface

The FA-66 is a very small (and therefore portable) FireWire audio/MIDI interface with a tough red metal exterior; it's Mac OSX and Windows compatible. It can be FireWire bus-powered, and includes a built-in limiter (for the inputs only). The front panel features two XLR/TRS combo inputs with phantom power and input sensitivity knobs, a Hi-Z (high impedance) button for the second input, a digital input select switch, direct monitoring knob and soft ctrl switch (for direct monitor control via ASIO software), stereo/mono select, phones socket, and master volume knob. The rear panel's got DC mains power in (for computers that don't provide enough bus power), power switch, 4- and 6-pin FireWire ports, sample rate select switch (from 44.1-192 kHz), phantom power switch, limiter switch, 4 1/4" phono outputs, MIDI in, MIDI out, S/PDIF digital in and out, phonos for inputs 3 and 4, and an input level knob for 3 & 4. The built-in limiter is a good idea – preventing distortion on incoming signals without having to use a separate hardware (or software) limiter.

The FA-66 doesn't need the computer to be shut down every time it's attached/detached to/from the computer; something which is required for M-Audio FireWire devices; if you're constantly packing/unpacking your gear (which I am), this quickly becomes annoying. The FA-66 doesn't have the most outputs – a maximum of 6 are available, depending on sample rates – but for musicians in small studios or doing small gigs, it's enough (DJs note – Live allows you to send Cue outputs to the FA-66's 3/4 outputs, but you'll need to add a mixer for headphone monitoring, unless you're a Mac user – see below). Good news for Mac users is that it's fully compatible with OSX's FireWire and MIDI drivers – no driver installation is required; at a recent gig I was able to lend the FA-66 to another PowerBook user, who was having problems with his own interface. It's an exercise in minimalism – small case, slim manual, no drivers (for Mac users) – and no software mixer for routing flexibility; this is something included with several other interfaces, but not everybody will miss it.

Use the Direct Monitor knob when you're recording an instrument into a Live set that already has some tracks with audio. The knob balances audio from the computer with any incoming signal. If you deactivate the receiving live track, it'll still record from the FA-66, but won't output any audio at all, that guarantees you're just hearing the FA-66 input. These can be useful features if you're dealing with latency problems, especially combined with Live's Device delay compensation, and Track Delay.

The FA-66 is a great box – it's been reliable in both studio and performance environments, and Live has never failed to recognise it. It's quite resilient – although it's not something that's recommended, there are times when I've forgotten to connect the FA-66 before launching Live, and I've plugged it in regardless, and Live has recognised it without problems. This kind of reliability definitely takes the pressure off in live situations! The only thing to beware of is that if you're already pushing your computer, then you add the FA-66 into the situation, you may experience clicks and other noises in your audio output. This is usually solved by using the FA-66's mains adaptor – taking the load off your computer.

Info

Choosing the right audio interface depends on what exactly you plan to do with it. The biggest problem is software drivers; if your system's working perfectly, avoid jumping on the latest driver update; let somebody else be the guinea pig! I've experienced some really frustrating problems relating to driver updates for audio interfaces – that's why, as a Mac user, I welcome the driver-free FA-66.

Combo audio/MIDI interfaces/controllers

FireWire audio/MIDI interfaces are now readily available; rarer are the true do-it-all devices that combine audio/MIDI interface and hardware MIDI controller. For examples of these see the Yamaha 01x, M-Audio Ozonic, and the M-Audio ProjectMix I/O. If you're building a system totally from scratch, one of these will cover all your needs in a single box, with just one cable required...jump to 'Using Live With Hardware Controllers' to read more about these.

Live and multiple audio interfaces

I'm showing my Mac bias again here. Live will only identify one audio interface at a time. However, OSX 10.4 (aka Tiger) recognises multiple audio interfaces, and combines them to create an 'aggregate' device with extra outputs - you can create various configurations and name/save them. Better still, the Mac's built-in audio system can be included as a device.

Launch Live, and the aggregate appears just like a regular audio interface. This is a way of using something like the FA-66 or X-Station to prelisten for DJing, even though they don't appear to support that in hardware. Send your master tracks out to the PA, and the cue output via the Mac's built-in audio, where you can listen to it on headphones.

(Right) Mac OSX aggregate devices panel

Aggregate device selection in Live preferences

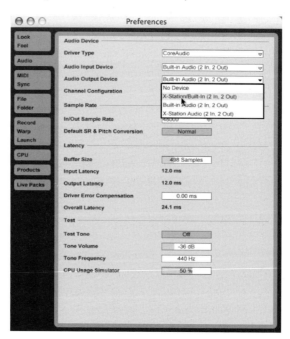

Specific aggregate outputs in Live's Session view

Get more sounds

The search for new sounds is never-ending, whether it's arrived at via a new effect, a sample, or a new software instrument. Here's some ways Live users can add new sounds to their collection...

Samples on disc
Sample discs range from modest audio CDs to host-specific DVD-ROM packages. No matter how hardcore you are about creating your own sounds, there are times when boil-in-the-bag samples, especially drum loops, are a real lifesaver. Composers working in commercial environments are especially grateful for this kind of themed sample collection – they make it easy to get an 'appropriate' groove going quickly. If you built an entire song just using untreated loops from sample CDs, it would be pretty sterile-sounding, but Live excels at sonic manipulation – the more you mangle, the better it gets! At the simplest level there are sample sets on audio CD, guaranteeing universal compatibility at low cost (there's a lot less preparation time involved for the manufacturer).

Info – iTunes is your friend
iTunes is the free music/video player/librarian from Apple, available for Mac OS and Windows – you probably have it on your computer already. iTunes' folders and playlists are just as good for organising loops and one-shots as they are entire songs. Direct one of Live's three File Browsers to your iTunes Music folder, or a sub-folder within that; if you're into DJing with Live, you can keep your pre-warped songs in an iTunes playlist, so you can easily access them from either application.

Tip
Drop your samples into iTunes making sure 'Copy files to iTunes Music folder when adding to library' is selected in iTunes Preferences/Advanced.

Live can grab tracks straight from audio CDs, and they'll be auto warped like any other material (make sure you save your set as self-contained afterwards, otherwise you'll be in trouble when you eject the CD).

If you're online when you insert a mass-produced audio CD in your computer and you have iTunes open, it'll get the song titles for you, and Live's Browser will update to display the same info. Drag your chosen song/s from the Browser straight into the Session or Arrangement View, then use Live's 'Collect All and Save' option to include a copy of the song/s when you save the Live set.

More expensive than audio CDs are format-specific discs (which can be CD or DVD). Where audio CDs contain straightforward loops and sounds, these discs contain ready-to-go software instrument banks and patches, as well as folders containing basic audio files. Live's basic samplers, Impulse and

Song loading and auto warping from CD

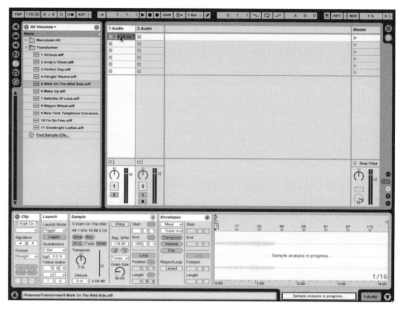

A fully auto warped song from CD

Simpler, don't support any major sample formats, but if you purchase the optional extra Sampler multisampler, you can import samples in many different formats including Akai, EXS, and Kontakt. You can of course use other AU or VST samplers, such as HALion and Kontakt.

Even if you don't have any third party sampler plug-ins, many sample packages contain their own interface, usually based on Native Instrument's Kontakt, so you don't need to already be a user of a particular sampling platform.

Online samples

Online libraries allow you to pick and choose individual samples, instead of buying entire discs; a good option if you just want to grab a quick sound effect or beat. Powerfx are 'old-timers' in this field now, and their site currently offers material in various styles including ambient, blues, classical, electronica, and hip hop, and in formats such as Acid, NNXT, EXS, HALion, Rex2, and Apple Loops. You should also check out The Freesound Project, which is (in their words) 'a collaborative database of Creative Commons licensed sounds'. The sounds available are quite diverse, but mostly focussed on electronic, field recordings, and experimental sources.

Apple Loops

Owners of GarageBand-equipped Macs will find their computers contain a number of Apple Loops (basically fancy AIFs, for Live's purposes), which can be drag'n'dropped straight into a Live set, and treated exactly like regular AIFs. If you install anything like Logic or Soundtrack Pro, you'll end up with thousands of these things.

...and Apple instruments

Even better for Mac users; because Live's Sampler can open EXS/Logic format sample instruments, you can use the GarageBand and Logic sample-based instruments that already live on your Mac. See our 'Sampling' chapter for more on this.

Reason Refills

You already know how Reason and Live can snuggle up close to each other, and how Live can share Reason's sounds via ReWire. As well as commercially-available Reason Refills from people like Time+Space, there are many free or cheap – and good – Refills available on the web; the only things I use Reason for these days. See Kreativ Sounds (their Analog BASStard is great), and Reason Banks (their Analog Monsters collections are must-haves for all Reason users).

Using Live with Stylus RMX

Spectrasonics' Stylus RMX is a good example of a third-party instrument plug-in; a drum module which runs as an AU, VST or RTAS. It installs a 7.4 GB sound library, and has a mixer page, and built-in effects, including compression, distortion, and delay. Up to 8 patterns can play simultaneously, whether full drum loops or individual percussion parts. Each of these 8 parts can be assigned to a separate stereo output – so, each can be routed to a separate Live track for mixing/processing. Although at times Stylus RMX is a bit of a monster (too much interface, if you see what I mean), it contains great material, in a more-or-less accessible format. Spectrasonics should be complimented on their support for RMX – there are HOURS of tutorial QuickTime movies, including specific information on using it with Live.

Assigning Stylus outputs to Live inputs

By default, RMX sends all 8 tracks to a master stereo output. However, it's easy to change this so that some or all of the tracks go to individual tracks in Live. Go to the Stylus mixer page, and load a drum part in each of the 8 tracks. Then click on the 'OUT A' box at the left of each track. It'll pop up a list from OUT A to OUT H. Assign each Stylus track to a different letter: A-H. Return to your Live window, and create 8 new audio tracks. For each one, select a Stylus output from A-H as the input source, then arm the track. Now you can apply Live's

Stylus RMX output selection

Stylus RMX outputs appearing in Live

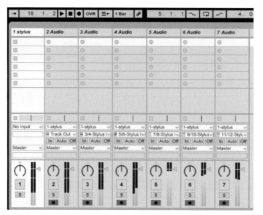

Stylus RMX part being dragged into Live

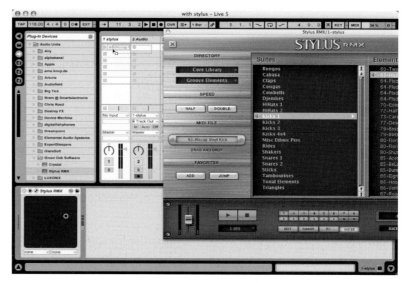

effects to individual Stylus parts, and of course record each part into a new clip within Live. Remember that you can also do this kind of routing exercise with Impulse!

If you're into beat driven music, you could do an entire slammin' live set with just Live and RMX – triggering beats and editing effects with a hardware controller like the Trigger Finger. It's also possible to edit RMX parts by dragging the selected part into a Live MIDI track and treating it like any other clip. Of course, Stylus beats are included in your stereo renders, just like with any other plug-in. You can't crack open RMX's audio content, but if there's a particular hit that you want to grab, trigger it from a controller, or Live's pseudo-MIDI keyboard, and record it into an audio clip, then drop it into Impulse to build an 'RMX' kit.

Live's own drum sampler, Impulse, is great – you don't need anything else, but if you insist on more drums, Stylus is a good way to go.

Trackteam Audio Livefills

Trackteam were the first to release CDs containing Live content (presets for instruments and effects, MIDI and audio clips) that install directly into the Live Library. They've even created lesson files that are accessed in the same way as Live's lessons, right in the Live interface itself. The Live-friendly range includes: Tacklebox, Travelbox, Beatbox, and Modmachines vs Breadbox. These sets are cutely-packaged (yes, that matters), very affordable, and highly recommended.

Ableton Live Packs

Ableton are now releasing their own Live Packs – collections of presets and Live Clips. These packs take advantage of the new Live Clip format introduced with Live 5, and install directly into the library, for immediate browsing. Hopefully Live Packs will allow Ableton to provide us with some provocative material, instead of the homogenous gloop that usually marks the widespread acceptance of a music application – how many Apple Loops do you need?

Add-ons like these will help us access more and better sounds, without having to ReWire to other applications – keeping everything within the familiar and functional Live interface. See Chapter 19 for more on Live Packs.

Operator

Operator was controversial on its initial release – its inclusion in demo form within Live 4.1 aggravated people who thought it should be cheaper (or free), and some objected to the fact that it was Live-specific, and couldn't be used within other sequencers. Operator has gone on to be appreciated as a

Operator

powerful creative tool that has the advantage of seamless integration with the Live environment. Operator is a great source of new sounds, and it's right under our noses; we just have to figure out how it works! Before you spend money on CDs or samplers, take the time to understand Operator, Impulse, Simpler, and Sampler; they shouldn't be underrated.

Info

My live set drums come from Impulse – apart from that I don't use any software samplers or instruments on stage, rendering everything as audio clips in advance – it's more flexible for performance, because then I can move clips between tracks more easily; it's also less demanding of my laptop.

Record your own

Live is a sampler. Record audio straight into it; mix and match sources – microphone/pre amp, your computer's built-in mic, minidisc, your phone, your iPod...Live rules in these collage-type situations. I love MacMice's MicFlex USB microphone, a mono USB mic on a flexible gooseneck-style metal arm (I mentioned it earlier in 'Performance Notes'). It slots into a desktop base, for that radio announcer vibe, or the flexible portion can plug directly into a free USB port; probably the most minimal way to add a microphone to your Live setup.

External sound generators

Live can send MIDI to control external synths or samplers. If you've got some old gear getting dusty in the corner – use it or sell it! For Live, this is effectively the same as communicating with other software – see Live's Preferences for MIDI/Sync settings, and remember you can send bank and program changes from MIDI clips.

External DSP cards

How about working with an external box like TC Electronics' FireWire Compact – the modern version of the hardware sound module? This one connects via FireWire, and integrates right into your computer setup, with each effect or instrument appearing as a plug-in. The Compact features useful studio effects such as compression and reverb, but also includes a synth based on the Roland SH101. The Compact is expandable, adding synths like the Access Virus and Novation V-Station. The Compact has no physical audio connections, just FireWire – the audio signal routes out of Live exactly as with any other plug-in. Tragically for laptop geeks like me, the Compact is not bus-powered!

TC Electronic Compact

Live packs

A Live Pack is a Live project which has been archived using Live's 'manage files' File menu item. Lossless compression techniques are used, which means the project can be reduced in size by up to 50%. The original project remains separate and intact, it's just like creating a .zip archive from a document or folder. Everything in the project is included in the Pack. This format is intended to allow smoother archiving of Live projects, to facilitate easier sharing between users, and to create handy packages for commercial or non-commercial distribution of Live content. Live Packs are an important part of Live's overhauled file management system, and we need to know how to use them...

You can obtain Live Packs from the Ableton website (for those who purchased the download, rather than boxed, version of Live), or from Live-using friends or contacts online. There are also commercial Live Packs available, from producers like Puremagnetik – they have a great selection of Packs available, including instruments, samplers, and device racks. If you purchased the boxed/disc version of Live 6, the Live Packs are on both installation discs – these comprise the EIC instrument collection mentioned elsewhere in this book. A Live Pack will have the file suffix .alp. There's a direct link to the Ableton website in the Live Packs section of Live's Preferences.

You can search for Live Packs using your computer's regular search functions (use '.alp' as a keyword), or from within Live itself – choose 'Install Live Pack' from the File menu, and navigate to your .alp files. If you know where the .alp file that you want is, double-click it – Live will launch if it isn't already open.

As your Live Pack launches, you'll be asked 'Would you like to install the Live Pack NAME'. Say yes. You can't go wrong – you can uninstall Live Packs later if necessary, and if you accidentally open a Live Pack that's already installed, you'll be notified, and the installation will be aborted. Any 'official' Ableton Live Packs will automatically be installed in the main Live Library. Live Packs from third parties – you, your friends, other producers – will require you to state where you want them to be installed. There's no specific requirement for this – just put them wherever you keep your Live projects.

So the time has come when you want to create your own Live Pack – maybe to share with a friend, or to post online to share with a wider community. What's in the Pack is up to you – it could be an entire Live project, with sets, samples, and presets, or any combination of those elements. From Live's File menu, choose Manage Files. This will open the 'Lessons view' window at the right of the screen. Amongst other things, you'll see a button

Manage Project view

called 'Manage Project' – click this. Live will then take a few moments to scan the current Live set, before giving you a detailed breakdown of info about the set – relating to project and sample locations and sizes.

You can use this list to locate missing samples, or to remove unused samples. In either case, the procedure is similar. To locate missing samples: if Live scans your set and discovers that a sample is missing, you'll see this message 'One sample used by this Project is missing.' with a Locate button below. Click the Locate button and you'll be presented with various search options – if you think you know where the sample is, navigate to it, otherwise make a choice from the options. Easiest way is to click the 'Go' button next to 'Automatic Search'. This may take some time, though, as Live will search your entire computer if necessary.

To remove unused samples: click on the 'Show' button in the Unused Samples list. The file browser at the left will open (this movement between browsers can be confusing, I know), and the unused sample or samples will appear – you can delete them from this list. This is a DELETE operation – if you want this sample for other projects, DON'T delete it!

Back in the Manage Project window (remember you can use the 'back' and 'forward' buttons if necessary to move between these windows), the 'Packing' item lower down the screen has a button 'Create Live Pack'. Click on this to begin the packing process. It will ask you where to save the Live Pack. If I'm creating a Pack to archive on a drive, or to send to somebody, I just save them to my desktop. How long the procedure takes will depend on how large your Live project is.

Once your Live Pack is created, it'll appear in your desired location with the .alp suffix. If you want to check it, there's no reason why you can't unpack it in the usual way – you'll be asked to specify a location for the unpacked file, just put it somewhere accessible, like on your desktop, and trash it once you've confirmed it works. Check out the size of the .alp compared to the original Live set – the lossless compression works!

Burn your Live Pack to CD, DVD, or post it online. Live Packs are not platform-specific – a Mac user can share his Packs with a Windows user.

Another thing you can do is use the 'Export to Library' option to copy all of the project's files in the Library – which is good if you want to keep them easily accessible for use in other projects.

The Live Packs tab in Preferences – displays a list of all installed official Live Packs on your computer, with relevant notes about each. To uninstall a Pack from this list, simply click on it, then use the 'Uninstall' button at the end of the page.

Links

Ableton www.ableton.com
You guessed it – makers of Ableton Live.

Ableton Live DJ www.abletonlivedj.com
Leading unofficial resource for Live-using DJs.

Apple www.apple.com
Desktop and laptop computers, GarageBand, Logic, Soundtrack Pro, iPod, iTunes; information on recording, podcasting, etc.

Audacity: http://audacity.sourceforge.net
Free audio editor for Mac OSX, Windows, and Linux.

Behringer www.behringer.com
Makers of FCB1010 MIDI foot controller, and various other MIDI control devices.

Behringer FCB1010 Yahoo Users Group
http://groups.yahoo.com/group/fcb1010
Support group for users of the FCB1010; this group makes all the difference between success and failure with your FCB.

Jen Bloom www.myspace.com/jenniferbloom
Live-using singer/songwriter/pianist, working out of New York.

Frank Blum www.frankblum.de
Live-using soundtrack composer.

Boss www.roland.com
Makers of GT-6B bass effects processor.

Circular Logic www.circular-logic.com
Makers of the InTime tempo sync system.

ControlAid www.charlie-roberts.com/controlAid
Incredibly useful MIDI routing utility for Mac OSX.

Cubase www.steinberg.net
Leading cross-platform 'traditional' DAW – digital audio workstation.

Echo Audio www.echoaudio.com
AudioFire2 DJ audio/MIDI interface.

Edirol www.edirol.co.uk, www.edirol.com
Various USB and FireWire interfaces and controllers.

Ergo Phizmiz www.ergophizmiz.com
Prolific Live user who loves to jam in the Arrangement View.

Faderfox www.faderfox.de
Extremely portable Live-specific MIDI controllers.

John 00 Fleming www.john00fleming.com
DJ...writer...Live user!

Freesound http://freesound.iua.upf.edu
Archive of sounds available under Creative Commons license.

GarageBand www.apple.com/garageband
Apple's low cost DAW, ReWire friendly.

Griffin Technology www.griffintechnology.com
PowerMate USB knob controller.

Hubi's MIDI Loopback
http://members.nextra.at/hubwin/midi.html
Popular MIDI routing utility

InStand www.instand.com
Innovative laptop stands suitable for performance use.

Jazz Mutant www.jazzmutant.com
The radical Lemur touch screen control surface.

J-Lab www.myspace.com/jlabmusic
Ableton Live-steeped laptop performer.

Junxion www.steim.org
Send MIDI with game controllers.

Kenton www.kentonuk.com
Builders of Killamix Mini USB MIDI controller.

Keith Lang www.songcarver.com
Live-using performer and software developer. See also: www.cocoajacksonlane.com, for info on Keith's band.

Logic www.apple.com
Apple's powerful DAW, in Express and Pro versions.

Mackie www.mackie.com
They do the Mackie Control Universal, a hardware control surface supported by Live.

M-Audio www.maudio.co.uk, www.m-audio.com
An enormous range of USB and FireWire audio/MIDI interfaces, controllers, etc. distributors of Ableton Live.

MDA www.mda-vst.com
Some of the best free AU and VST plug-ins around.

MidiO http://home.comcast.net/~retroware RetroWare
AU plug-in which allows GarageBand to send MIDI to applications such as Live.

MIDI Ox www.midiox.com
Self-proclaimed 'world's greatest all-purpose MIDI utility'.

MIDI Yoke www.midiox.com
MIDI patching utility.

mindlobster www.mindlobster.com
Live-obsessed laptop performer and producer with highly visual live show.

MOTU www.motu.com
828, Traveler and Ultralite audio interfaces.

Musolomo www.plasq.com
Innovative plug-in sampler instrument.

Native Instruments
www.nativeinstruments.com
Software: Absynth, B4, FM7, Kontakt, Pro53, Reaktor.

Nintendo www.nintendo.com
Wii Remote Control.

Novation www.novationmusic.com
The Remote25 and Remote SL MIDI controllers.

Nusystems www.nusystems.co.uk
Pre-installed music computer systems, laptop and desktop varieties.

OSC www.opensoundcontrol.com
Multi media control protocol, designed to 'replace' MIDI.

PC Publishing www.pc-publishing.com
They published this book!

Pluggo www.cycling74.com
Plug-in suite, but not like all the rest! Cycling 74 are now collaborating with Ableton.

PowerFX www.powerfx.com
Online and on-disc resource for audio samples in various formats.

Pro Tools www.digidesign.com
The pro's DAW.

Public Loop www.publicloop.com
Pioneering educational project based around Ableton Live and Arkaos VJ.

Puremagnetik www.puremagnetik.com
Producers of Live Packs.

RadiaL www.cycling74.com
Loop-based performance software from the Pluggo people.

Raidius www.raidius.com
FinalKeys computer keyboard overlays – make your own Live controller template.

Reason www.propellerheads.se
Reason self-contained software studio, an excellent sound source for Live.

Spectrasonics www.spectrasonics.com
Stylus RMX, AU/VST drum unit.

Tacklebox www.trackteamaudio.com
-Add-on packs of presets and samples for LIve's instruments.

Jesse Terry http://music.download.com/jethro
Live/FCB1010-using artist.

Time+Space www.timespace.com
Major providers of virtual instruments, sample CDs, etc.

WiiToMidi http://mike.verdone.ca/wiitomidi
Mike Verdone's freeware application which allows the Wii Remote Control to communicate with music software, including Live.

Jody Wisternoff www.wayoutwest.uk.com
Jody's from Way Out West, the Bristol-based DJs/remixers/producers.

Yamaha www.yamahasynth.com
01x audio-MIDI interface/controller/mixer, compatible with Live via Mackie Control support.

Joe Young www.theplaysthething.com
Live-using composer, working in theatre and dance.

Hans Zimmer www.hans-zimmer.com
Live-savvy Hollywood soundtrack whiz.

Top ten keyboard shortcuts

Some of these are keyboard shortcuts that I use a lot and some are ones I should use a lot... (showing Windows/Mac versions).

1	Tab	toggle Arrangement and Session
2	F11/Ctrl F11	enter/exit full screen
3	Shift-F12	show/hide Track/Clip View
4	Ctrl l/Cmd l	create loop from selection (also activates loop button if not already on)
5	Right-click/Ctrl-click	show context menu
6	Ctrl k/Cmd k	Key Map Mode
7	Ctrl m/Cmd m	MIDI Map Mode
8	Ctrl-shift-k/Cmd-shift-k	computer MIDI Keyboard on/off
9	Ctrl j/Cmd j	consolidate
10	F1-F8	activate/deactivate tracks 1-8

Index

aggregate device, 134
Apple instruments, 137
Apple Loops, 136
Arkaos VJ, 76, 85, 119
Arrangement View, 3, 62, 66
Arrangement, 65
audio audio clip automation, 59
    clips, 3, 32, 53
    hardware, 15
    interface, 132
    recording with audio effects, 50
    sample stretching, 60
    multiple audio clips, 29
    multiple audio interfaces, 134
    routing between tracks, 38
    routing, 13
Audio Effects, 45
Auto Filter, 87, 107
automating the cross fader, 61
automation, 57
Auto-Warp, 98
auto-warping, 32, 87

Back to Arrangement, 63
band, using Live in, 84
Behringer FCB1010 MIDI foot controller, 125
BPM changes, 37
    scene changes, 75
Browser, 15, 18

Capture And Insert Scene, 37
Chain List, 79
Chain Select Zone, 79
Channel Configuration, 15
classroom, 107
Clear Envelope, 62
clips, 25
    audio, 32, 53
    deactivate, 30
    clip envelopes, 26
    clip groove pop-up menu, 26
    MIDI, 33
    multiple audio clips, 29

    clip nudge, 57
    song setup clips, 68
    clip start and end markers, 25
Clip RAM Mode, 17
Clip Scrub Control, 25
Clip View, 30
Collect All and Save, 16, 22
colour-coding, 28
Complex warp mode, 32, 87, 90
compression, lossless, 141
computer keyboard mapping, 72
consolidation, 17, 29
context menu, 14, 34, 126
Control Chooser, 80
ControlAid, 127
creating a rack, 49
Crop Sample, 22
crop sample, 30
cropping, 17
crossfader, 89
    automating, 61
cueing, 88
    DJ style, 132

DAW, 75
deactivate clips, 30
deactivate notes, 35
Delete Envelope, 62
Demo Mode, 12
Device Chooser, 80
device delay compensation, 50
device racks, 6, 45, 49, 57
    in a live situation, 78
devices, 45
DJs, 87
Draw Mode, 57
drum machine, 55
drum sampler, 55
DSP cards, external, 140
Dynamic Tube, 45

Echo AudioFire 2, 88, 132
Edirol FA-66 FireWire, 133
Enigma, 125, 129

149

Envelope View, 80
EQ Eight, 45
EQ3, 87
Essential Instrument Collection, 7
export, 105
    MIDI, 35
EXS/Logic, 137
external DSP cards, 140

fast MIDI mapping, 542
FCB1010, 70
file management, 8
    sizes, 16
File Browser, 21
File Management browser, 23
follow actions, 30
Frank Blum, 104
freeze tracks, 78, 84

GarageBand, 118
global groove option, 26
Griffin Technology PowerMate, 130
groove, 26

hardware, 13
    audio, 15
    controller, 123
    MIDI, 15
    MIDI hardware setup, 88
hot-swap, 56
Hubi's MIDI LoopBack, 67

IAC Bus, 67, 68
Impulse, 47, 53, 55, 78
Info View, 6
Install Live Pack, 141
installation, 11
Instant Mapping, 125
Instruments, 45
iTunes, 90, 135

Jazz Mutant Lemur, 129
Jen Bloom, 96
Jesse Terry, 127
J-Lab, 81
Jody Wisternoff, 88

Keith Lang, 84
Kenton Killamix Mini, 123, 132
Key Map Mode, 36, 107
keyboard, 123
    pseudo-MIDI, 131
    shortcuts, 147
Killamix Mini, 123, 132

Lessons, 13, 49
Library, 19, 64
links, 143

Live Clips, 25, 32
Live within a band, 84
    for DJs, 87
    in the theatre, 85
Live Library, 18
Live Packs, 19, , 23 139, 141
Live's Lessons, 13, 49
load sets or parts of sets, 21
locators, 84, 105
Locators, 93
Logic, 48, 116
loop bracket, 29
lossless compression, 141

Mac, 11
    OSX IAC Bus, 67, 68
Mackie Control Universal, 127
Macro knobs, 79
Manage Files, 23, 141
Manage Project, 142
Manage Sample File, 22
Mapping Browser, 128
mapping
    computer keyboard, 72
    MIDI, 71,
mashups, 96, 98
M-Audio
    Ozonic, 77, 128
    Trigger Finger, 124
metronome, 33
MicFlex USB microphone, 139
MIDI clip automation, 58
    clips, 3, 33
    controllers, 58, 69
    effects, 46
    exporting, 35
    hardware, 15
    hardware setup, 88
    interface, 132
    mangler, 70
    mapping, 71
    mapping, fast, 54
    note quantization, 34
    multiple MIDI controllers, 126
    routing, 13
    track, 67
MIDI clock, 111, 122
MIDI Editor, 35
MIDI Effects, 45
MIDI Map Mode, 10, 36
MIDI Ox, 67, 127
MIDI Timecode, 111, 122
MidiO, 118
movie soundtracks, 103
moving to Live, 20
MTC, 122
multiple audio clips, 29
multiple audio interfaces, 134

multiple MIDI controllers, 126
Multisample Mode, 55
Musolomo, 84

Nintendo Wii Remote Control, 129
Note Length, 45, 46
notes, deactivate, 35
Nudge, 25

Open Sound Control, 129
Operator, 47, 48, 119, 127, 139
OQ8, 6
OSC, 129

PC, 11
pencil tool, 57
Powerfix, 136
pre-analysis, 90
pre-listing, 88
Preview, 35
Program Change Select box, 121
project folder, 22
pseudo-MIDI keyboard, 131

quantization, 34
QuickTime movie, 103
　　integration, 8

rack, creating, 49
Reason, 47, 51, 111
Reason Refills, 137
record quantization, 34
remix/mashup, 98
remixes, 98
renaming a clip, 25
render without recording, 112
Re-Pitch warp mode, 87
rewire slave, 114
ReWire, 31, 46, 106, 111
routing, 8
　　audio and MIDI, 13
　　audio between tracks, 38

sample discs, 135
Sampler, 6, 47, 49, 53, 55, 136
Sampler filer, 56

sampling, 53
Save Current Set as Template, 17
scenes, 35
　　song header, 38, 77
Scrub Area, 95
Select Next Scene on Launch, 37
Session, 65
Session View, 1, 3, 25, 65, 120
Session View mixer, 8
sets, 21
shortcuts, 14, 147
Simpler, 47, 48, 53, 54
songs song header scenes, 38, 77
　　song setup clips, 68
　　warping, 90
Songcarver, 84
songwriting, 95
Status Bar, 131
Stylus RMX, 137
Swap Browser, 8
system requirements, 11

tap tempo, 90
Tarekith, 89
TC Electronics FireWire Compact, 140
templates, 17
theatre, using Live in, 85
track freeze, 93
track freezing, 8, 78, 84, 93
Trackteam Audio, 138
troubleshooting, 77

unlink, 63
　　envelopes, 26
Utility, 46

Video Window, 104
Vintage Warmer, 51

warping, 3
　　entire songs, 90
Warp markers, 8
WiiToMidi, 129

16-step sequencer, 100